MOSES MAIMONIDES'
TREATISE ON RESURRECTION

AN INQUIRY INTO ITS AUTHENTICITY

BIBLIOTHECA MAIMONIDICA

TEXTS, STUDIES AND TRANSLATIONS
IN MAIMONIDEAN THOUGHT AND SCHOLARSHIP

edited by

JACOB I. DIENSTAG

VOLUME I

STUDIES IN
MAIMONIDES AND ST. THOMAS AQUINAS

VOLUME II

ESCHATOLOGY IN
MAIMONIDEAN THOUGHT

VOLUME III

MOSES MAIMONIDES'
TREATISE ON RESURRECTION

MOSES MAIMONIDES'
TREATISE ON RESURRECTION

AN INQUIRY INTO ITS AUTHENTICITY

by

LEA NAOMI GOLDFELD

KTAV PUBLISHING HOUSE, INC.
NEW YORK
1986

Library of Congress Cataloging-in-Publication Data

Goldfeld, Lea Naomi.
    Moses Maimonides' treatise on resurrection.

    (Bibliotheca Maimonidica ; v. 3)
    Bibliography: p.
    Includes index.
    1. Maimonides, Moses, 1135–1204. Maḳ'alah fī
teḥiyat ha-metim. 2. Resurrection (Jewish theology)
I. Maimonides, Moses, 1135–1204. Maḳ'alah fī teḥiyat
ha-metim. English & Hebrew. 1986. II. Title.
III. Series.
BM645.R47M334   1986   296.3'3   86–7499
ISBN 0–88125–088–0

Manufactured in the United States of America

לאמי

הרבנית בלה פוגלמן זכרונה לברכה

הלכה לעולמה ביום כ"ט אב תשל"ה

לאבי

הרב ד"ר מרדכי פוגלמן זכרונו לברכה

הלך לעולמו ביום ט' אלול תשמ"ד

Contents

Acknowledgments

I would like to express my gratitude and appreciation to Dr. J.L. Teicher, who opened before me new directions of thought, taught me so much, and did not weary of guiding me.

I owe a great deal to Mrs. G. Burkill, who encouraged me in every way, and whose sincere efforts made it possible for me to study at the University of Cambridge.

To the Burney Fund Committee, Divinity School, Cambridge, I owe many thanks for their kind and generous financial assistance.

I am extremely grateful to the staff of the Cambridge University Library, and to the staff of the Library of the Faculty of Oriental Studies for facilitating my research.

To the Tel-Aviv University Central Library, I wish to express my thanks for the resources which were made available to me.

Finally, my thanks to my husband, who helped me through all the years of study, and to my children, whose understanding meant a great deal to me.

Cambridge,
Wolfson College,

Introduction*

In chapter ten of Tractate *Sanhedrin* of the Mishnah it is stated: "Those who have no share in the Hereafter (*ᶜolam ha-ba*) are: He who maintains that the resurrection of the dead is not derived from the Torah . . ."[1]

A passage in the *Mishneh Torah* reads: "In the Hereafter neither a body nor a bodily shape exists, but the souls of the righteous without bodies . . ."[2]

The *Treatise on Resurrection*[3] has: "It seems to us that those whose souls return to their bodies will eat and drink and die again . . . after a very long life . . ."[4]

There is a general agreement in Jewish literature that the *Treatise on Resurrection* was written in Arabic, by Maimonides (d. 1204), the author of *Mishneh Torah.*[5] The general assumption of non-Jewish literature is that Maimonides has two conflicting opinions on the subject of resurrection, namely, that in the *Treatise* he expresses his belief in physical resurrection, while in *Mishneh Torah* he ignores physical resurrection by giving an exclusively spiritual interpretation of the Hereafter.[6]

RAbaD, a talmudic scholar from Posquières (d. 1198), interpreted Maimonides' silence as a denial of physical resurrection and first took issue with him over it.[7] Possibly during Maimonides' lifetime, his statement in Chapter Eight about a purely spiritual existence in the Hereafter became the center of a controversy which continued until far into the thirteenth century. The first phase of the controversy was marked by the burning in Montpellier, ca. 1234,[8] of some of Maimonides' books, the *Book of Knowledge,* which is the first part

---

*The transliteration of the Hebrew is according to the rules of *Encyclopaedia Judaica* (Jerusalem, 1971), slightly modified.

The transliteration of the Arabic is according to the *Encyclopaedia of Islam.*

The translation of the Hebrew text is my own, except when otherwise stated.

1

of *Mishneh Torah* (known also as *Yad ha-Ḥazaqah,* Maimonides' Code), and the philosophical work, the *Guide of the Perplexed.*

The existence of a *Treatise on Resurrection* ascribed to Maimonides did not prevent Shem Tov ben Yosef Shem Tov (d. 1440), of the opposing school of thought, from writing: "And we have come to the conclusion [which we derive] from [Maimonides'] opinions, that what the French Rabbis, among others, understood . . . is true and correct . . . namely, that he [Maimonides] did not believe in a physical resurrection . . ."[9]

That is to say, in spite of the publicity that the *Treatise* had gained by that time, it was still difficult to reconcile the opinions of the author of the *Treatise*[10] with the opinions of the author of the *Book of Knowledge.* However, doubts of the authenticity of the *Treatise* were not raised in any of the known sources which referred to it. The classical commentators on Maimonides' *Mishneh Torah*[11] try to find a compromise between Maimonides' opinions as expressed there and their own conceptions, without making any comment on the *Treatise.* The critical edition of the *Treatise* by J. Finkel points to various problems in the Hebrew and Arabic manuscripts of the *Treatise,* but the question of its authenticity is not touched. The first scholar to question its authenticity was J. L. Teicher.[12] His purpose was to show that the *Treatise* "is an important document, which strongly reflects the trend to Christianization of the Jewish religion which had started just then in France."[13] His conclusions are: The *Treatise* was originally written in Hebrew during the second half of the thriteenth century. Maimonides was not the author, and the ideas expressed in it are basically different from the ideas of Maimonides as expressed in *Mishneh Torah* and the *Guide of the Perplexed.* In his introduction to a Hebrew edition of the *Treatise,*[14] M. D. Rabinowitz wrote that although the arguments given by J. L. Teicher are extremely convincing, they are revolutionary, and therfore instead of going into the details of scholarly research, one should accept the *Treatise* as genuine. Another reaction to J. L. Teicher's work is from S. W. Baron,[15], who asserted that Teicher has indeed proved that the original treatise was written in Hebrew and that the edition of the Hebrew text of the *Treatise,* by Finkel, is not an Ibn Tibbonic translation. Further, the edited Arabic text was not written by Maimonides, but is a translation from the original Hebrew text. S. W. Baron, who agrees with J. L. Teicher, expresses the hope that he will find additional proof for his thesis. A dissident opinion is expressed by I. Sonne,[16] who disagrees with Teicher's method of arguing and presents the problems under discussion in a rather subjective way. He makes no comment, however, on the internal contradiction of the *Treatise,* as contained in the two claims that the resurrected will die again, quite apart from any question of the Hereafter, and that physical resurrection is the precondition for reward and punishment in the Hereafter. This contradiction is the crux of the matter. Sonne maintains that one has to accept the *Treatise* as a simple letter which is addressed to the general public and not to philosophers. He reaffirms Maimonides' authorship of the *Treatise,* although he acknowledges that not all that Maimonides wrote is so clear as to preclude any doubts. It seems that S. W. Baron, who at first intended to accept J. L. Teicher's argument that the *Treatise* is spurious, has changed his mind, and now considers the *Treatise* to be genuine.[17] Thus, the question of its authenticity remains.

Our task will be to reexamine the whole question of the authorship of the *Treatise on Resurrection,* hitherto attributed to Maimonides.

Tehiyyat ha-metim is the Hebrew term for "resurrection of the dead." The traditional non-Jewish as well as Jewish definition of "resurrection of the dead" denotes the actual rising of a dead person from his grave. The Hebrew term meaning "the revival of the dead" is open to more than one interpretation. *Tehiyyah,* or *tehayah* (as in the Yemenite tradition), is a verbal noun (*shem ha-po'al*) from *hiyyah,* the *pi'el* conjugation. It is derived from the root *hyh, hyy.*[18]

Three conjugations of this root are observed in biblical and talmudic sources:

1. *Qal* (*hay*), meaning: to live (Gen. 42:2); to exist (Deut 8:3); to recover health (2 Kings 8:8); to revive from death (2 Kings 13:21).

2. *Pi'el* (*hiyyah*), meaning: to let live (1 Kings 20:31); to give life (Hos. 14:8); to restore life to the dead (Ps. 30:4).

3. *Hif'il* (*heheyah*), meaning: to let live (Josh. 14:10); to preserve (*B.T.*

Baba Meẓia 88b); to restore life to the dead (2 Kings 8:1, *J.T. Berakhot* 9:3); to recover from illness (Isa. 38:16). *Tehiyyah* usually appears in talmudic literature (*J.T. Soṭah* 9:15, *Sanhed.* 10:11, *Kiddush.* 39b, *Bera.* 5:2) in the expression *Tehiyyat ha-metim,* and in liturgic Hebrew in the *piˁel: mehayyeh ha-metim,* and *le-hahayot metim* in the *hifˁil.*

In the light of these grammatical details, it seems possible to understand *tehiyyat ha-metim* in several ways; for example: survival, revival, resurrection. In attempting to define its exact meaning, we shall examine closely each text under consideration, keeping in mind the different possible meanings.

    Tehiyyat ha-metim, as a term, does not appear in the Bible. This fact is emphasized in the Talmud,[19] where midrashic exegesis is used to demonstrate its derivation from the Torah. The Talmud does not give a definition of the term "resurrection," and there is no halakhic rule on it. Joseph Albo, the Spanish philosopher (15th cent.), reviews the different possible meanings of *tehiyyat ha-metim.* He says: "We may say that the expression 'resurrection' in this place denotes the reward of the soul and its life in the world of souls. . . . They (in the Talmud) call it resurrection of the dead in opposition to the Sadducees."[20]

    It seems that the belief in future resurrection penetrated into Judaism from outside,[21] and that it became a part of the mixture of ideas associated with the Messiah, the Day of Judgment, and the Hereafter. It is therefore impossible to speak of a "talmudic view on resurrection."

    Tehiyyat ha-metim is the central motif of the second benediction in the main daily Jewish prayer, the *shemoneh ˁesreh.*[22] It would not be easy for us to decide now what the meaning of *tehiyyat ha-metim* was at the time when the term was introduced into the Jewish liturgy.[23] We know, for instance, from the New Testament[24] that the Sadducees denied the resurrection of the dead, while the Pharisees believed in it.[25] But this does not help us to know what the Pharisees meant by it. The New Testament is quite clear on the importance of belief in resurrection[26]: "If Christ be not risen, then is our preaching in vain, and your faith is also in vain."

It would seem that under Christian rule, Jews were encouraged to believe in resurrection. A Novella of the Emperor Justinian, edited in 553,[27] reads: "But if any one of them [the Jews] dare introduce godless and vain teachings denying the Resurrection, the Last Judgment, or that the angels are the work and creation of God, it is our will that that one shall be expelled from every place. . . . those who dare say such things shall be subjected to the most severe penalties so that we may thereby purge the Jewish people of this error." This Novella is a "historical document of the first magnitude."[28] From it we learn that the subject of resurrection was not an integral part of Jewish thought in the sixth century, nor did this subject play any important role in the worship in the Synagogue. The decree of Justinian was imposed on the Jews who were under the rule of the Byzantine Empire, and who possibly tried to teach the denial of resurrection. It might be suggested that the term "resurrection" was understood by the Jews as being open to two conflicting interpretations. It is possible that tehiyyat ha-metim had a twofold meaning,[29] that is to say, a spiritual and a physical meaning. It is to the latter that certain Jewish communities objected.

A comprehensive survey of the history of the belief in resurrection is outside the scope of this work. The points that are mentioned here are only a few milestones in the history of a complicated theological conception.

The non-Jewish religious background of Maimonides was that of the Moslem world, to which the religious Christian imposition in matters of belief and heresy was alien. J. Finkel suggests that the attitude of the Islamic orthodoxy during Saladin's reign might have caused Maimonides to write the Treatise.[30] He mentions the critique against Maimonides' philosophic work.[31] There is no evidence, to our knowledge, in the Treatise itself or in other historical documents,[32] that a certain Islamic view or pressure could have been Maimonides' reason for writing the Treatise. Maimonides was free to express his views and theological beliefs. This he did in Mishneh Torah, where he connected his philosophical-theological conception with the Jewish law, the Halakha.

The great Muslim theologian and mystic, Ghazālī (d. 1111), accepting the literal meaning of the Qurʾān, opposes the philosophers who deny, among other doctrines, bodily resurrection, and accuses them of heresy.[33] Two generations later, Ghazālī was criticized and refuted by the most important Aristotelian, Ibn Rushd (d. 1198). Asserting that the philosophers believe in the necessity of religious law, Ibn Rushd points out that "all religions agree in accepting another existence after death, although they differ in the description of this existence."[34] He, however, rejects physical resurrection, holding that "it must be admitted that the soul is immortal, as can be shown by rational and religious proofs, and it must be assumed that what rises from the dead is simulacra [images, substitutes] of these earthly bodies, not these bodies themselves, for that which has perished does not return itself but can only return as an image of itself, not as being identical with what has perished, as Ghazālī declared."[35]

In *Mishneh Torah* Maimonides deals with every aspect of the rules of Halakha. Many subjects that had not previously been considered halakhic matters by the talmudic scholars are included in the *Book of Knowledge,* which opens the *Mishneh Torah.* One of these subjects is the belief in the immortality of the soul in the Hereafter. For Maimonides, this belief is part of the Halakha, to be studied and accepted by everyone, and not restricted to the periphery of philosophy. Physical resurrection is implicity excluded from Maimonides' concept of the Hereafter.

The main idea of the *Treatise on Resurrection* is that physical resurrection will take place after death and both the body and the soul will be rewarded or punished for their previous life.

The question we have to answer is whether Maimonides is likely to have held this idea. We will, therefore, reexamine the text of the *Treatise on Resurrection,* taking into consideration both those problems which have been dealt with elsewhere and those which we raise for the first time.

Our first effort will be to ascertain, as far as is possible, what was Maimonides' explicit notion of the eschatological eon. i.e., of the Hereafter, the Resurrection, and the Messianic era. We shall then go over the text itself in detail, taking it section by section, and try to show why it could not have been written by Maimonides. In order to do so, we shall have to go into the controversy which raged round the question of what Maimonides really thought. This will include editing a text from a talmudic commentary known as *Yad Ramah*. *Yad Ramah* is an important part of our study. As far as we know, there has been no discussion in scholarly research on this particular part of *Yad Ramah,* which itself seems to be part of a Commentary of *Pereq Ḥeleq. Pereq Ḥeleq* is a chapter of Tractate *Sanhedrin. Yad Ramah* contains a long quotation from the *Treatise on Resurrection.* We shall try to establish the connection between *Yad Ramah* and the *Treatise on Resurrection.* In addition to the quotation from the *Treatise,* this text reveals many aspects of the above-mentioned controversy, includes details which have a bearing on the historical background of the *Treatise,* and discusses at length the Hereafter, the Day of Judgment, Resurrection, and the Messianic era, citing the Talmud as its authority. A careful analysis of the text of *Yad Ramah* might lead us to a new approach to the problematic *Treatise on Resurrection.*

Notes

1. In some versions, for instance the Cambridge MS edited by W. H. Lowe, the words "from the Torah" (the Law) are missing.

2. Moses ben Maimon, *Mishneh Torah,* henceforth referred to as *M.T. Book of Knowledge, Hilkhot Teshuvah* (rules of repentance), chap. 8, henceforth referred to as Chapter Eight.

3. Moses ben Maimon, *Ma'amar Tehiyyat ha-Metim.* Maimonides' *Treatise on Resurrection,* henceforth referred to as the *Treatise.*

4. *Treatise,* par. 23.

5. M. Steinschneider, *Hebraeische Uebersetzungen,* p. 431.

6. M. Joseph, *Encylopedia of Religion and Ethics,* vol. 11, p. 147.

7. *Mishneh Torah ʿim Hassagat ha-RAbaD,* Chapter Eight.

8. Z. Graetz, *Divrei Yemei Israel,* vol. 5, p. 63. S. Kook, *Kirjath Sepher,* vol. 1 (1925), p. 160, reprinted in his *ʿIyyunim u-Meḥkarim,* vol. 2 (1963), p. 172–73.

9. Shem Tov, *Sefer haʾEmunot, Shaʿar rishon, pereq ʾalef,* p. 1.

10. The *Treatise* is quoted in Moses ben Naḥman's *Torat ha-ʾAdam, Kol Kitvei* (ed. C. Chavel), vol. 2, p. 309. Albo alludes to its contents in *Sefer ha-ʿIqqarim,* vol. 1, p. 54; vol. 4, p. 290 (ed. I. Husik). Abravanel, for instance, mentions it in *Naḥalat ʾAvot,* p. 61b. See also E. Pocock, pp. 86ff., on "Judaeorum sententia de resurrectione mortuorum" in *Notae.*

11. Joseph Caro, *Kesef Mishneh,* on *Mishneh Torah, Book of Knowledge, Hilkhot Teshuvah,* Chapter Eight. Shem Tov ben Abraham, *Migdal ʿOz.,* Meir ha-Kohen, *Haggahot Maimoniyot.*

12. J. L. Teicher, *Melilah,* vol. 1 (1944), pp. 81–92.

13. Ibid., p. 92.

14. Moses ben Maimon, *ʾIggerot,* p. 213.

15. S. W. Baron, *Hatequfa,* vol. 30–31, pp. 825–26.

16. I. Sonne, *PAAJR,* vol. 21, pp. 101–17.

17. S. W. Baron, *Social and Religious History,* vol. 5, p. 296, n. 22; vol. 8, p. 312, n. 24.

18. Ben Yehuda, s.v.

19. *B. Sanhedrin* 90b.

20. Albo, *Sefer ha-ʿIqqarim,* vol. 4, p. 306 (trans. I. Husik).

21. I. F. Baer, *Israel ba-ʿAmim,* p. 35; J. Gutmann, *Philosophies of Judaism,* p. 14.

22. "Thou revivest the dead" is a part of the second benediction, known as *gevurot* (force, might). *B. Berakhot* 21b, 29a–b, 33a; *B. Megilah* 17b. See also I. Baer, *Seder ʿAvodat Israel,* and the *Authorized Daily Prayer Book.*

23. One of the midrashic interpretations is that the dead will be revived by *ṭal* (dew). *B. Ḥagigah* 12b.

24. Acts 23:8.

25. See also Josephus, *Antiquities,* XVIII, 13–16.

26. 1 Cor. 15:14, 23. The medieval Jewish point of view is that the Christians "place alongside reward and punishment the coming of the Messiah and the resurrection of the dead. Without these it is clear that their religion cannot exist." Albo, *Sefer ha-ʿIqqarim* (trans. I. Husik), vol. 1, p. 201.

27. P. E. Kahle, *The Cairo Geniza,* p. 316.

28. Ibid., p. 39.

29. W. Marxsen, *Resurrection,* p. 135.

30. Finkel, p. 71.

31. Ibn Abī Uṣaybiʿa, *ʿUyūn al-anbāʾ, fī ṭabaqāt al-atibbāʾ,* p. 687: "He (Maimonides) also composed *a book for the Jews* . . . . I saw it and found it a vile book which weakens the roots of laws, etc."

32. Ibn Khallikān, *Wafayāt al-Aʿyān,* vol. 2, pp. 261–63, on the biography of Shihāb al-Din al-Suhrawardī, a Muslim mystic philosopher executed in Aleppo. Some of the reasons given for his execution were: boasting among friends that he would become the ruler of the world; denial of the omniscience of the Creator; too much interest in certain "ancient philosophers."

33. Ghazālī, *Tahāfut,* pp. 229ff.

34. Averroes' *Tahāfut,* vol. 1, p. 362.

35. Averroes, *Kitāb faṣl al-maqāl,* p. 17, says that to deny resurrection is heresy because it is a branch of the law. The uneducated must accept it literally, and to reveal its esoteric meaning to them is heresy because it leads to heresy.

1

Maimonides' Opinion on Eschatology

In *Mishneh Torah,* the *Book of Knowledge, Hilkhot Teshuvah,* Chapter
Eight, Maimonides says: "The good which is in store for the righteous is the life of the Hereafter.[1] That good is a life which is free
from death, and that good [is a life] that is free from evil. This is
what the Torah[2] says: 'That it may be well with thee, and that thou
mayest prolong thy days.'[3] [Our] oral tradition explains [that verse
as follows]: 'That it may be well with thee' in a world that is entirely
good; 'and that thou mayest prolong thy days' in a world that is
everlasting. That [world is] the Hereafter.[4] The righteous are
rewarded by achieving that pleasure [the pleasure of the life of the
Hereafter] and [they are also rewarded] by [being able] to exist in
that good. [On the other hand], the wicked are punished by [being
unable] to achieve that life [of the Hereafter]. [The wicked] will be
cut off and will die. Everyone who does not achieve that life [of the
Hereafter] is dead forever.[5] This means that he is cut off because of
his wickedness and he is lost in the same way as an animal is. This is
the meaning [of the expression] *karet* (being cut off) that is used in
the Torah:[6] 'Cutting off *(hikkaret)*; [That soul] will be cut off *(tikkaret).*'[7] Our oral tradition teaches: '*Hikkaret* [means] in the [physical]
world, *tikkaret* [means] in the Hereafter.'[8] In the Hereafter neither a
body nor a bodily shape[9] exists. Only the souls of the righteous
[exist in the Hereafter], disembodied like the ministering angels.
Since there are no bodies [in the Hereafter] there is no eating nor
drinking. [The Hereafter] does not contain anything that human
bodies need in our world. None of the things which happen to
bodies in our world, such as: sitting, standing, sleep, death, sorrow,
laughter, or the like happen there. This is what the first sages said:
'In the Hereafter there is no eating or drinking and no copulation,
but the righteous sit with their crowns on their heads, and feast on

9

the brightness of the divine presence.'[10] Therefore, it has been made clear to you that no bodies exist there, because there is no eating or drinking. The saying 'the righteous sit' is allegorical. It means that the righteous exist there [in the Hereafter], without toil and without endeavor. The expression 'their crowns on their heads' refers to the knowledge which they had acquired, which knowledge [enabled] them to attain the life of the Hereafter. They retain it [in the Hereafter] and [that knowledge] is their crown. As Solomon said:[11] '. . . the crown wherewith his mother has crowned him.'[12] And he [the prophet] says: 'And an everlasting joy upon their head.'[13] But joy is not an object to be worn upon the head any more than is the crown about which the sages spoke, [which] means knowledge. And what does the saying 'feast on the brightness of the divine presence' mean? [It means] that they [the righteous] know and understand the truth of God[14] [in a way] which is incomparable to what they can know while still [existing] in an earthly and base body. Whenever the [term] soul (*nefesh*) is mentioned in connection with that subject [the Hereafter], it does not refer to the soul (*neshamah*) which inhabits a body, [but it refers to] the form of the soul (*zurat ha-nefesh*), which is [itself] the knowledge that understood the [idea of the] Creator, depending on its [degree] of ability to do so. . . That life [of the Hereafter] is free from death, since death belongs to the things which happen to the body, and there is no body there. [That life] is called 'a bundle of life.'[15] This reward is the ultimate reward and the good after which no other good can [have value]. That [good] was longed for by all the prophets."

Maimonides continues to explain: "The [reason why] it is called by the sages *ha-ʿolam ha-ba* (the Hereafter) is not because it [the Hereafter] does not exist now, [namely], that the [present] world will be destroyed, and [only] then, that world [the Hereafter] will take place. This is not so. [The Hereafter] is [already] present and exists [now], as it is said: '. . . which thou hast laid . . . which thou hast wrought.'[16] [The sages] called it *ʿolam ha-ba* only for the reason that life comes to a man after the life in the [physical] world, in which we exist through body and soul, and which is bestowed upon every man at first."

The above passages from Chapter Eight furnish us with

Maimonides' teaching on the halakhic ruling about *ʿolam ha-ba*. The Hereafter is one of the subjects that are dealt with in the *Book of Knowledge*, which opens Maimonides' main work on Jewish law. The *Book of Knowledge* discusses matters of faith which are in Maimonides' view a part of the religious law, the Halakha. According to Maimonides, the fundamental article of religious belief is the knowledge that God exists and that He is the Creator of the universe. He who imagines that there is another God is denying a principle "which is the greatest principle on which everything else depends."[17] The knowledge of God, states Maimonides, leads at the end of one's physical life to the life of the Hereafter. The righteous who were able to advance in the knowledge of God will have the privilege of reaching the life of the Hereafter. That privilege is the only kind of reward for the righteous, after their death. The life of the Hereafter means the eternal survival of the soul. In contrast to that reward is the punishment of the wicked, before whom the gate to the Hereafter is shut. They are doomed to be totally dead, like animals, their souls unable to reach any level of understanding of the idea of God. Their souls are excluded from the life of the Hereafter. This exclusion is in itself the punishment of the wicked, who have no survival whatsoever. One would have expected Maimonides to express his opinion about physical resurrection in a chapter devoted to the future of the human individual after his death. However, Maimonides does not discuss the subject of resurrection at all. Chapter Eight states that the life of the Hereafter is free from three factors: death, evil, and the physical existence of bodies. That life cannot be compared to anything known to us from our experiences in this life. Maimonides cites his proof from the traditional interpretation of the biblical verse "that it may be well with thee, and that thou mayest prolong thy days."[18] He accepts this source as evidence for the everlasting good life of the Hereafter. On the same lines Maimonides maintains that the verse "cutting off; that soul will be cut off"[19] is to be accepted according to its traditional interpretation of the twice-emphasized verb, to be cut off. The wicked will be destroyed bodily and spiritually in this world. Their physical death is the very end of their existence, their souls will perish with their bodies, which in itself is the punishment for their wickedness. The

life of the Hereafter is free from death and from evil anf from any of
the factors which make up physical existence in the world. What
remains of the human individual is the soul, which no longer needs
a body.[20] This is made clear by Maimonides when he refers to the
passage that reads: "In the Hereafter there is no eating or drinking
. . ."[21] Maimonides explains that because of the lack of food in the
Hereafter there is no possibility for the body to exist. The second
part of the quotation, "but the righteous sit with their crowns on
their heads, and feast on the brightness of the divine presence," is
understood by him alegorically. It is not, he holds, that righteous
really sit, according to the usual meaning of the verb *y sh v*. The
same applies to "their crowns on their heads," which is to be understood as a pictorial parable. The correct meaning of the phrase is
that the righteous exist in the Hereafter without the toil which is
part of life in this world, and the "crowns" express the knowledge
which the righteous had acquired when alive and endowed with
souls as well as bodies. "Feast on the brightness of the divine
presence," Maimonides explains that the righteous are more able to
grasp the idea of God, by being in the Hereafter, than they did in
this world. The Hebrew term *ha-ʿolam ha-ba,* the Hereafter, which
verbally means "the world to come," has a clear and definite meaning in Maimonides' view. The Hereafter exists in the present and is
not separated from this world. It is called "the Hereafter" not
because it will come into existence after this world is ended, but
because the righteous enter into its life immediately after they have
died in this one. In other words, for the body death is the end, but
for the soul it marks the transition from this world to another life.
Maimonides teaches that *ʿolam ha-ba,* the Hereafter, is the life that
comes (*ha-baʾ lo la-ʾadam*) to that individual who is worthy of it.
Maimonides, clearly does not draw a dividing line between the con-
cepts of *ha-ʿolam ha-zeh,* this world, and *ha-ʿolam ha-ba.* By this he
deviates completely from the traditional distinction between two separate worlds.

In chapter nine of *Hilkhot Teshuvah,* Maimonides explains the
meaning of the Messianic era (*yenot ha-mashiah*), and makes a clear
distinction between that era and the *ʿolam ha-ba,* the Hereafter. The
Messianic era is a period of worl ly history which has no connection

with the Hereafter. The Messianic era, which will take place in the future, is not a part of any eschatological event. Whatever happens in the Messianic era will fall into categories of earthly events. A specific feature of that time is the change in the political situation of the Jewish nation, i.e., the rebuilding of an independent state, which will lead to prosperous economic conditions. Such conditions of life will help those who live at the time to be able to concentrate more and more on the study of the Torah. The more the people are able to study the Torah and perform its precepts, the more they will be able to achieve a knowledge of God, which in its turn will lead them to the life of the Hereafter. But this is the only connection between the pleasant life of the people during the Messianic era and the better chance for those people to be able to reach higher levels of knowledge of the divine truth, which knowledge secures for them an eternal spiritual life. The same idea is dealt with at length at the end of *Hilkhot Melakhim* (rules of kings), which concludes *Mishneh Torah*. We shall refer to this subject at a later point in our work.

Another aspect of a traditional view of the Day of Judgment is not touched upon by Maimonides in *Hilkhot Teshuvah*. He does not mention *yom hadin,* the Day of Judgment, in connection with *ʿolam ha-ba.* Maimonides does not make divine judgment dependent on the Day of Judgment, which notion is alien to Maimonides. Divine judgment depends only on repentance.[22] The Hereafter is in itself the reward for the righteous as a result of their knowledge of God. The fact that the wicked are cut off (*karet*), and are unable to live the life of the Hereafter, is in itself a form of divine justice. Neither reward nor punishment is dependent on the Day of Judgment.

Maimonides is completely silent on the subject of the resurrection of the body. There is no explicit denial of the possibility of bodily resurrection. On the other hand, he states that there is no corporeal existence in the Hereafter, which means that the existence of the body in the Hereafter is not a precondition for the existence of the soul after this life. The text of Chapter Eight leads us to the following conclusion: Maimonides believes in the survival of the soul after death, which is called by him "the life of the Hereafter." Only the righteous can reach that eternal life, which is a reward for their knowledge of God. The wicked have no survival, their souls perish at their death, which is their punishment. Corporeal resurrection is not mentioned. He is positive that the Hereafter exists in the present for the righteous who depart from this life, which means that the immediate survival of the soul does not need a resurrected body. If this is so, Maimonides does not leave any period of time for bodily resurrection. Therefore, it is understood, implicitly that Maimonides does not believe in resurrection of the body. The Hereafter always exists for the individual, and it is not connected with any historical period, in contrast to the future era of the Messiah, which is an expected historical event.

These opinions of Maimonides in Chapter Eight sowed the seeds for a controversy about his attitude toward the belief in bodily resurrection.

Maimonides' contemporary, Rabbi Abraham ben David (RAbaD), who had objections to the *Mishneh Torah,* says in connection with Maimonides' statement that "in the Hereafter neither a body nor a bodily shape exists," the following:[23] "The words of that man [Maimonides] seem to me to be like saying (*kemi she᾽omer*) that there is no resurrection of bodies but only of souls. I swear that this is not the opinion of the sages, as they said in *Ketubot:*[24] "In the future the righteous will arise in their clothes . . ."[25] and as they said:[26] "All those [sayings] prove that they rise to life in their bodies. God might make (*yasim*) their bodies strong and healthy as the bodies of the angels and the body of Elijah . . . while the [meaning] of the crowns [should be interpreted] literally, and not as an allegory." RAbaD represents a certain school of thought in Judaism that accepts the midrashic exegesis of the verbal meaning of biblical verses. RAbaD will not acknowledge any allegorical interpretation, as for instance, the interpretation that Maimonides gave to the word "meal,"[27] which, according to the midrash, is awaiting the righteous in the future. Maimonides maintains that this is one of the allegorical descriptions of the Hereafter. In that case, says RAbaD, in his pungent criticism: "If this be 'the meal' there would be no cup over which to say grace. He [Maimonides] would have been better silent [about the matter]." RAbaD has a different opinion about the *῾olam ha-ba.* He maintains that in the future,[28] another world, a new one, will exist after the chaos that will be the end of the present world. In

RAbaD's opinion, Maimonides rejects the whole idea of another world. RAbaD accepts the literal meaning of the passage:[29] "Six thousand years the [present] world lasts, one [thousand years] it is a waste." Whereas in the *Guide of the Perplexed* we find a different explanation of the same sentence. Maimonides' conception that the world is eternal is stressed by the following deduction: "the passing-away of this world, a change of the state in which it is, or that a thing is changing its nature and with that the permanence of this change, is not affirmed in any prophetic text or any statement of sages either. For when the latter say, 'the world lasts six thousand years, and one thousand it is a waste,' they do not have in mind total extinction of being. For the expression, 'and one thousand years it is a waste' indicates that time continues. Besides it is the saying of an individual that corresponds to a certain manner of thinking."[30] In Maimonides' view, there exists only one world, and it is eternal, comprising also the *ʿolam ha-ba,* the Hereafter.

It seems that Maimonides knew about his contemporary, RAbaD, who became famous in the world of Jewish learning through his criticisms of, and objections to, *Mishneh Torah.*[31] Nevertheless, no direct comment was made by Maimonides in answer to those objections.[32] RAbaD's assertion seems to be the first reaction to Maimonides' silence on physical resurrection. In the whole *Mishneh Torah,* the term "resurrection of the dead" (*teḥiyyat ha-metim*) appears only once:[33] "And those who do not have a share in the Hereafter, but are cut off (*nikhratim*), destroyed, and condemned for ever and ever in consequence of the nature of their wickedness and sinfulness, are: the *minim* [dissenters], the *epiqorsim* [epicureans], those who reject the Torah, the resurrection of the dead, and the coming of the redeemer."[34] Maimonides gives as his source a paragraph from the Talmud.[35] This paragraph deals with the harshest sanction in Judaism, known as the *karet.* It means that those liable to *karet* forfeit their share in the life of the Hereafter. We shall refer to this passage again at a later stage of our discussion (p. 37), but we would like to point out now that the term "resurrection of the dead" is not defined or given any clarification in the subsequent explanatory passages.

The term *meḥayyeh ha-metim* appears in *Mishneh Torah* at the end

of the *Book of Love,* where, in the section "Order of the Prayers for
the whole year," Maimonides lists the eighteen benedictions of the
daily prayers. The second benediction contains several repetitions of
the phrase *mehayyeh metim.* This benediction could refer to the survival of the spirit only, and thus poses no particular questions for us.
There is, however, one instance which we must go into more fully.

In *Mishneh Torah, Hilkhot Tefillah* 7:3, Maimonides cites certain
benedictions which appear in the regulations of the sages in Talmud
Bavli, *Berakhot* 60b. Maimonides writes as follows: "When the sages
authorized the wording of these prayers, they authorized additional
benedictions to be said every day." He continues by giving these
benedictions, but uses his own wording: "When he [a man] wakes
up, at the end of his sleep, he says when still on his bed the following:[36] 'Oh my God, the soul which Thou gavest me is pure; Thou
didst create it, Thou didst form it, Thou didst breathe it into me;
Thou preservest it within me; and Thou wilt take it from me, but
will restore it unto me hereafter. So long as the soul is within me, I
will give thanks unto Thee, O Lord my God and God of my fathers,
Sovereign of all works, Lord of all souls! Blessed art Thou, O Lord
who restorest souls unto the dead.'" In the light of this liturgical
passage, which is a quotation from the text of the prayers as they
appear in the Talmud, it is difficult to pinpoint Maimonides' views
on the meaning of the phrase "wilt restore it unto me hereafter." It
is possible to say that the very fact that Maimonides quotes this particular passage from the Talmud proves that it is also his own
opinion, namely, that a physical resurrection will take place.

But on the other hand, there is a variant in MS Oxford 80, fol.
105 r, at the end of which appears Maimonides' attestation in his
own handwriting (fol. 165 r), that that MS was revised on the basis of
his own copy of the *Mishneh Torah.*[37] The reading of the preposition
is different. The text of the benediction is: "Thou wilt restore it *to
me*" and not "*into* me," the last being the accepted text in the printed editions.

Therefore it is possible to explain that Maimonides aims at the
spiritual survival of the individual's soul. While the preposition "*into
me*" (*bi*) means something that enters into me, inside me, the preposition "to me" (*li*) means something that is transferred *to me,* exter-
nally, but does not change my inside.

From here it can be understood that the meaning of the benediction "Thou wilt restore it *to me*" (*li*) as it appears in the variant of the
above-mentioned Oxford MS could be interpreted as a spiritual
survival only.

The correctness of the variant *li,* which appears in MS Oxford
80, is also borne out by the fact that there are parallels of the same
variant in some MSS of the Talmud. Note no. 40 in *Diqduqei Soferim*
on *B. Ber.* 60b mentions as one of these parallels a MS which was
copied in the book *Beit Nathan* (the book includes variants on Tractate *Berakhot* based on an old MS that was brought from Egypt to
Jerusalem). It might well be that Maimonides used the same or a
similar source for the talmudic excerpt in his Code. Furthermore,
the correctness of the variant *li* becomes even more probable when
we read the counterpart of the same benediction: "O Lord who
restorest souls *unto* the dead" (this is the English translation in the
Authorized Daily Prayer Book, 2d rev. ed. [London, 1962], p. 6). The
phrase here is *ha-mahazir neshamot li-fgarim metim* and not *bi-fgarim
metim*. This is also the variant of the preposition *li,* which appears in
all the parallels of the talmudic texts, and not *bi,* namely, "to the
dead" and not "into the dead."

As to the contents of the morning benediction, I would like to
add that Maimonides says clearly that that benediction should be
said "when [a man] wakes up, at the *end* of his sleep, when still on his
bed." Maimonides rules that "there is no [established] sequence for
these benedictions. One should say each of them topically and temporally adapted to its subject" (*Hilkhot Tefillah* 7:5). Therefore, it
would seem that to Maimonides this benediction was topically and
temporally connected with waking up in the mornings.

The benediction under discussion expresses several ideas. Two of
these are: the belief of the prayer in the survival of the soul, and his
gratitude for the daily waking up from sleep. The last phrase,
"restorest souls unto the dead," or literally, "restorest souls unto
lifeless corpses," seems to me a poetical description of the everyday
restoration of the soul to a new lease of life. In my opinion, this
benediction has no bearing on eschatological resurrection from
physical death. There is something common to sleep and death—
and this is the main idea expressed in "restorest souls unto the
dead" used in the morning benediction.

In conclusion, it should also be noted that the author of the
Treatise on Resurrection quotes every possible instance in Maimonides'
Code from which the idea of bodily resurrection might be deduced.
The above-mentioned benediction is not quoted. This should mean
that the author did not consider this source to hold any argumenta-
tive importance at all.

Up to now we have discussed Maimonides' opinion on eschatology as expressed in his halakhic work. Although he does not explicitly deny a future corporeal resurrection, his silence on the subject
and the way in which he explains the term *ha-ʿolam ha-baʾ*, the Hereafter, lead one to the conclusion that he did not believe in physical
resurrection.

We shall try now to find out what Maimonides says on the subject in his philosophical work, the *Guide of the Perplexed*.

Among the several possible definitions which Maimonides gives
for the word "air" (*ruaḥ*) is the following:[38] "Air . . . is also a term
denoting the thing that remains of man after his death and that does
not undergo passing away.[39] For example, 'And the air[40] shall return
unto God who gave it.'"[41] The same applies to the definition that is
given by Maimonides for "soul" (*nefesh*):[42] "And it is a term denoting the thing that remains of man after death, for example: 'Yet the
soul of my lord shall be bound in the bundle of life.'"[43] In connection with his definition of "living" (*ḥay*), Maimonides explains
"death" (*mavet*) on the same lines: "Living . . . is also a term denoting both death and severe illness."[44] He continues with an allegorical explanation of biblical passages containing the term "life"
(*ḥayyim*):[45] "I made a similar interpretation of His dictum, may He
be exalted, 'That ye may live,'[46] analogous to the traditional interpretation of the dictum of Scripture: 'That it may be well with
thee,[47] and so on. Because this figurative sense is generally accepted
in the Hebrew language, the sages said: 'The righteous even in death
are called living, [whereas] the wicked even in life are called dead.'[48]
Know this." The life of the Hereafter, or as Maimonides puts in in
the *Guide*:[49] "Correct opinions (*deʿot*) are called 'life' and false opinions [are called] 'death' . . . God, may He be exalted, says accordingly: 'See, I have set before thee this day life and good,' and so on
[and death and evil]."[50] Maimonides closes his discussion of the

term "living" by quoting the Talmud: "The righteous even in death are called living," a phrase which is not used by him in Chapter Eight, but is quoted in the Introduction to the Commentary on *Perek Ḥeleq,* with which we shall deal later (p. 26). However, Maimonides' definitions of the terms "living," "life," and "death" do not bring us closer to his own view on physical resurrection, on which he maintains silence in the *Guide*. The term "resurrection of the dead" itself is vaguely referred to when a midrashic exegesis of the verse "The rider in the *ʿaravot*"[51] is quoted by Maimonides.[52] The meaning of the verse, according to Maimonides, is: "He who dominates the highest heaven encompassing the universe."[53] The adjectives that are used in the Talmud[54] to describe the "highest heaven" are understood by Maimonides as an allegorical description: "*ʿAravot*—that in which [exist] righteousness, right-dealing, justice, the treasure of life, the treasure of peace, the treasure of blessing, the soul of the righteous, the soul and the spirits that shall be created in the future, and the dew by means of which the Holy one, blessed be He *will revive the dead*." "Not one of all the things enumerated here," says Maimonides, "is a *body* and therefore to be located in a place." Maimonides continues to explain very clearly that "the dew (*ṭal*) is not the dew denoted by the word in its literal meaning (*kifshuṭo*)." Although he does not say what the sages meant by "revive the dead," it is to be deduced from the general approach of Maimonides to the whole text that none of it is to be understood literally, and the same applies to the revival of the dead. In order to get a complete view of Maimonides' opinion on the matter, we quote the following passage:[55] "Consider that they said in this passage: 'That in which'—I mean to say that the things mentioned are in *ʿaravot*—and they did not say that the things are upon it. Thus they have, as it were, given the information that these things which exist in the world, exist only because they proceed from coming from the *ʿaravot* of God, may He be exalted, who caused [the *ʿaravot*] to be their first origin and who situated them in it. To these things belong the 'treasure of life.' In fact it is correct and absolute truth to say that every life existing in a living being only proceeds from that life [this is the meaning of the expression 'treasure of life'], as I shall subsequently mention.[56] Reflect also that they enumerated in the list 'the soul of the righteous ones, and the souls and the spirits that shall be created in the future.' How sublime is this notion to him who has understood it. For the *soul (neshamah)* that remains *after death* is not the soul that comes into being in man at the time he is generated. For that which comes into being at the time a man is generated is merely a faculty consisting in preparedness, whereas the thing after death is separate from matter, is the thing that has become actual and not the soul that comes into being; the latter is identical with the spirit that comes into being. Because of this [the sages] have numbered the souls and spirits among the things that come into being. What is separate is, on the contrary, one thing only. We have already made clear the equivocality of the term spirit.[57] We have already made clear, in the last portion of the *Book of Knowledge,*[58] the equivocality regarding these terms." Maimonides alludes here to Chapter Eight, where he explicitly says that only the soul reaches the life of the Hereafter, and this happens in the moment of one's physical death, a conception that does not leave any space of time for bodily resurrection. The clear distinction between the soul, which needs a body for its existence, and the form of the soul (*zurat ha-nefesh*), which survives after the body and its own soul have perished, leads to the conclusion that the soul that lives eternally is completely independent of the body, the eternal life being its reward. In Maimonides' view, bodily resurrection cannot be regarded as a reward for the righteous, and it cannot constitute a factor in the punishment of the wicked—the reason being, it seems, that it is absurd to revive the wicked in order to punish their bodies. This being so, there is no room for bodily resurrection.

In part three of the *Guide,* Maimonides introduces the rational meaning of the precepts of the Torah. His general rule is: "The Law (*Torah*) as a whole aims at two things: the welfare of the soul and the welfare of the body." The welfare of the soul means to Maimonides the ultimate perfection of the individual, which is "to have an intellect *in actu;* this would consist in his knowing everything concerning all the beings that it is within the capacity of man to know in accordance with his ultimate perfection." Maimonides asserts that "it is clear that to this ultimate perfection there do not belong either actions or moral qualities and that it consists only of opinions toward which speculation has led and that investigation has rendered compulsory. It is also clear that this noble and ultimate perfection can only be achieved after the first perfection has been achieved (i.e., the perfection of the body). . . . Once the first perfection has been achieved, it is possible to achieve the ultimate, which is indubitably more noble and is the only cause of permanent preservation (*hayyim matmidim*)."[59] This is, according to Maimonides, the life of the Hereafter, which is an integral part of the world. In Chapter Eight he calls it "the good that is in store for the righteous." In the *Guide* it is called the ultimate perfection which leads to a permanent existence, the existence of the soul. "The letter of the Torah speaks of both perfections and informs us that the end of this Law in its entirety is the achievement of these two perfections. For He, may He be exalted, says: 'And the Lord commanded us to do all these statutes (*huqqim*) to fear the Lord our God, for our good always, that He might preserve us alive, as it is at this day.'[60] Here He puts the ultimate perfection first because of its nobility; for . . . it is the ultimate end. It is referred to in the dictum: 'For our good always.' You know already what [the sages], may their memory be blessed, have said interpreting His dictum, may He be exalted: 'That it may be well with thee in a world that is entirely good, and that thou mayest prolong thy days, in a world that is an everlasting [world].' And this is perpetual preservation. On the other hand, His dictum: 'That He might preserve us alive, as it is at this day refers to the first and corporeal preservation, which lasts *for a certain duration* and which can only be well ordered through political association. . . .'[61] The same opinion is expressed in Chapter Eight, and in many more details in the last chapter of *Hilkhot Melakhim*,[62] where Maimonides speaks about the political meaning of the Messianic era with regard to the Jewish people.

In the third part of the *Guide,* Maimonides sums up his opinions about the true knowledge to be achieved by a human individual. "The true human perfection," says Maimonides, consists in the acquisition of the rational virtues—"I refer to the conception of intelligibles, which teach true opinions concerning the divine things. This is [in true reality] the ultimate end; this is what gives the individual true perfection, a perfection belonging to him alone; and it

gives him permanent perdurance; through it man is man."[63] The
ultimate end is "the knowledge of God, this is the true wisdom."
"The sages . . . apprehended from this verse ['Let not the wise man
glory in his wisdom . . . but let him that glorieth glory in this that he
understandeth and knoweth Me']⁶⁴ . . . that the possession of the
treasures acquired, and competed for, by man and thought to be
perfection are not a perfection; and that similarly all the actions pre-
scribed by the Law—I refer to the various modes of worship and
also the moral habits that are useful to all people in their mutual
dealings—that all this is not to be compared with this ultimate end
and does not equal it, being but preparations made for the sake of
this end." Can there be a greater contrast between this philosophical
view of Maimonides and the belief in bodily resurrection? At the
height of his discourse Maimonides emphasizes: "It is clear that the
perfection of man that may truly be gloried is the one acquired by
him who has achieved, in a measure corresponding to his capacity,
apprehension of Him . . ." According to this view, resurrection of
the dead, a physical resurrection, has nothing in common with the
ultimate end. In the light of the above passages from the *Guide,* it
would seem that Maimonides did not believe in physical resurrection, which, in his philosophy, is rendered pointless. The teachings
of Chapter Eight, as well as the conclusions from the above-quoted
passages from the *Guide,* stand in sharp contrast to the conclusions
which are derived from the *Treatise on Resurrection.* The *Treatise* states
that at a certain time in the future the soul will return to the body,
and this is what the expression "resurrection of the dead" means.⁶⁵
Maimonides' conception is that the soul of the human individual is
a part of the nature of the universe, a part of the whole structure of
the world, which was created from nothingness. The soul of the
righteous continues to live its own life, which is the life of the Hereafter. This is so although there is no doubt about the passing away
of the physical body, a process that belongs to the course of nature.
The world as a whole will continue to exist forever, as will the souls
which achieve that stage of life. Maimonides holds that the universe
was created from nothingness, and that it will last forever. "The
belief in the creation of the world (*ḥiddush ha-ʿolam*) is necessarily the
foundation of the entire Law. . . . Perhaps you will say: Has it not

been demonstrated that everything that comes into being passes away? If so, then the world that is generated will pass away. Know then, that need not apply to us. For we do not assert that it has been generated according to the rule applying to the generation of the natural things that follow a natural order. For what is generated in accordance with the course of nature must of necessity pass away in accordance with the course of nature. . . . However, in view of our claim, based on the Law, that things exist and perish according to His will, may He be exalted, and not in virtue of necessity, it is not necessary for us to profess in consequence of that opinion that when He, may He be exalted, brings into existence a thing that had not existed, He must necessarily cause this existence to pass away. Rather does the matter inevitably depend on His will: If He wills, He causes the thing to pass away; and if He wills, He causes it to last. . . . It is accordingly possible that He should cause it to last forever and to endure as He Himself. . . ."[66] This conception of eternity "applies to the souls of the virtuous; for according to our opinion, they are created, but will never become nonexistent. According to certain opinions of those who follow the literal sense of the Midrashim, their bodies will also be in a state of perpetual felicity for ever and ever—an opinion resembling that of those whose belief as regards the inhabitants of Paradise is generally known." From this passage of the *Guide,* it is possible to sum up Maimonides' implicit opinion on the resurrection of the dead. The world is eternal and so are the souls of the righteous, whom he calls, in the above passage, "virtuous." These souls remain eternal and would not change their eternal nature to become souls that return, presumably, into their bodies, which had already passed away. It is very likely that Maimonides' allusion in the above paragraph to "those who follow the literal sense of the Midrashim" and "whose belief as regards the inhabitants of Paradise is generally known" refers to those who uphold the view that Adam and Eve would have lived forever, both in body and soul, if they had not committed the sin of disobeying God. Maimonides' own view on the nature of Adam and Eve's sin is entirely different, and it is clearly expounded in the *Guide* I, chapter 2.

We would like to continue by discussing Maimonides' attitude toward the subject of the creation of the world (*ḥiddush ha-ʿolam*), showing how that subject is linked not only with the problem of the eternity of the world and the eternity of souls, but also with the subject of miracles. In the *Treatise on Resurrection,* the phenomenon of bodily resurrection is treated as a miracle,[67] thus justifying belief in bodily resurrection. But this is not the case in the *Guide of the Perplexed.* The question is if it can be deduced from the *Guide* whether or not Maimonides believed in miracles. His method in explaining the term *ḥiddush ha-ʿolam,* which means, according to his theory, the evolution of the universe, is built on the axiom that the world was created in the beginning. His description[68] of *ḥiddush ha-ʿolam* is a description of the universe during its evolutionary stage, until the universe reached the final stage of completion. This is based on the analogy of the embryo in the uterus of its mother, where the evolutionary stage occurs, i.e., until the physical structure is completed, until the child becomes independent. On the same lines, the universe reaching the final stage of completion, has every faculty in it, which means that no fundamental changes will take place anymore, thus excluding the possibility of miracles. This process is eternal: "A thing does not change its nature in such a way that a change is permanent," but we must "be cautious with regard to the miracles.[69] For although the rod was turned into a serpent, the water into blood, and the pure and noble hand became white [leprous] without a natural cause that necessitated this, these and similar things were not permanent and did not become another nature. But as they, may their memory be blessed, say: 'The world goes its customary way.'"[70] Maimonides explains that these miracles occurred due to necessity, in temporary circumstances. He acknowledged in this way the miracles that are reported in the Bible: "This is my opinion and this is what ought to be believed."[71] He believes that "what exists is eternal . . . that nothing in it will be changed in any respect unless it be in some particular of it miraculously—although He, may He be exalted, has the power to change the whole of it."[72] "However," says Maimonides, "that which exists has had a beginning, and at first nothing at all existed except God. His wisdom required that He should bring creation into existence at the time He did it, and that what He has brought into existence should not be annihilated nor any of its natures changed except in certain particulars that He willed to change; about some of these we know, whereas about others that will be changed in the future we do not know. This is our opinion and the basis of our Law."[73] Maimonides accepts the miracles of the Bible, which were witnessed by the people. A miracle, according to Maimonides, is a new, unexpected event directly produced, from the human point of view, by God's creative power for a single special occasion. The duration of such miracles, unlike natural, constant behavior, is temporary. The miraculous event has a special purpose which is always an event that helps the preservation of the people or of individuals. Resurrection is a constant state with no purpose, and it cannot be a miracle. Maimonides' doctrine of miracles excludes the notion of the *Treatise* that resurrection of the dead belongs to the realm of miracles.[74] Miracles do not contradict the laws of phenomenological nature because these laws are the result of divine creativity, just as is, on a larger scale, the evolutionary stage of the universe. Maimonides supports his theory about the evolution of the universe and the constant, established behavior of natural bodies by a "very strange statement about miracles[75] that was made by the sages: 'Rabbi Jonathan said: The Holy One, blessed be He, has posed conditions to the sea: [to wit], that it should divide before Israel. . . . Rabbi Jeremiah . . . said . . . He has posed conditions not only to the sea, but to all that has been created in the six days of the Beginning.'[76] This notion," says Maimonides, "consists in their holding the view that miracles, too, are something that is, in a certain respect, in nature. They say that when God created that which exists and stamped upon it the existing natures, He put into these natures that all the miracles that occurred would be produced in them at the time when they occurred." Maimonides emphasizes the importance of that statement made by the sages: "The superiority of the man who made it and the fact that he found it extremely difficult to admit that nature may change after the 'work of the Beginning' or that another volition may supervene after that nature has been established in a definite way, [is rather obvious]." Miracles, according to Maimonides, are not dependent on a certain personality, for instance a prophet or the Messiah. The hypothetical question "Why did He [God] privilege the prophet

with the miracles mentioned in relation to him and not with some
other [miracles]"[77] has one answer only: God wanted it this way.
"Every prophet that will appear . . . does not have to perform a
miracle similar to those miracles which Moses our teacher [per-
formed], or to miracles that [were performed] by Elijah and Elisha,
because [this means] a change in the course of the nature of the
universe . . . one should not ask the [prophet] to divide the sea or
raise someone from the dead."[78] A similar idea is expressed by
Maimonides in respect to the functions of the Messiah, who is not
expected to resurrect or to perform any miracles.[79] We have seen
that in *Mishneh Torah* and in the *Guide of the Perplexed,* Maimonides
dissociates the subject of resurrection from the subject of the Hereafter.

In his Introduction[80] to the Commentary of the Mishnah on
Tractate *Sanhedrin,*[81] chapter ten (known as *Pereq Ḥeleq*), Maimonides
gives the following statement: "And the resurrection of the dead is
one of the fundamental articles [of faith in the Law] of Moses,
blessed be his memory. He who does not believe in it possesses
neither religion nor adherence to the Jewish religion. But it (resurrection) is for the righteous only.[82] This is how *Bereshit Rabbah* has it:
'(*gevurat geshamim*) rain falls alike on the righteous and the wicked,
but the resurrection of the dead is for the righteous only.'[83] And how
will the wicked live since they are already dead in their lifetime?
They [the sages] said: 'The wicked even in their life are called dead
[and the] righteous even when they are dead are called alive.'[84] Know
that a human being must die, and be discomposed and return to the
elements out of which he was made." The subject of resurrection is
discussed among those of Paradise, Hell, and the Messianic era, in
the main part of the Introduction, which also deals at length with
the meaning of the Hereafter (*ʿolam ha-ba*). But the term "resurrection of the dead" remains unexplained in the same Introduction.

We assume that the term *teḥiyyat ha-metim,* which is mentioned in
the foregoing text, alludes to a spiritual revival or survival of the
soul and not to a corporeal resurrection. This assumption is possible because Maimonides does not explain the meaning of the term
but stresses the importance of the belief in *teḥiyyat ha-metim.* On the
other hand, we are confronted with a difficulty when explaining why

Maimonides, having discussed at length the meaning of ʿolam ha-ba, adds another statement on teḥiyyat ha-metim. If we assume that the meaning of teḥiyyat ha-metim is, according to Maimonides, the survival of the soul, why does he mention teḥiyyat ha-metim separately? I cannot find a solution to this puzzle.

We can also assume that the midrashic exegesis "[the righteous even when they are dead are called alive]," which appears in the Introduction to the Commentary, has the same allegorical meaning as in the Guide,[85] namely, that the "life" of the righteous refers to the life of the Hereafter.

The end of the Introduction includes Maimonides' test of the Thirteen Principles of the Jewish faith. The last sentence of this text reads: "And the thirteenth principle [is] the resurrection of the dead (teḥiyyat ha-metim), which we have already explained."

This brief statement seems to call for some comment.[85] Can it be that Maimonides alludes here to two former instances in the Introduction; the passage that states that a Jew must believe in teḥiyyat ha-metim, and the passage which emphasized the importance of ʿolam ha-ba, the Hereafter?

The thirteenth principle, as it stands, is not self-explanatory, but Maimonides offers us no help.

We would like to conclude our discussion of Maimonides' opinions on physical resurrection with a quotation from his preface to his general Introduction to his Commentary on the Mishnah. He is speaking about the death of Moses: "What happened to [Moses] when he ascended to the mountain of Nevo [without ever returning from it] has for us the significance of 'death' because he is gone from us (ḥasarnu ufaqadnu ʾoto). But [it] meant 'life' for him, because of the high standard he had achieved. That is why [our sages] said: 'Moses did not die, but he ascended the heights and he is serving in heaven.'[86] And the explanation of these matters is very long, and this is not the place for it."[87] And indeed, this was not the place for Maimonides to develop his theological-philosophical reasoning, which later on came to full and mature expression in his Mishneh Torah and in the Guide of the Perplexed. It was in these two works that he established the individual eschatology of the future, the constant life of one's soul. The idea about the miraculous physical resurrection, which is the motif of the *Treatise on Resurrection,* contradicts the nature and the essence of Maimonides' halakhic and philosophic opinions.

Notes

1. Literally: The world to come. I have throughout used the term "Hereafter" as the translation of *ʿolam ha-ba.*

2. The Mosaic Law.

3. Deut. 22:7.

4. *B. Kiddushin* 39b, *Ḥulin* 142a.

5. Hebrew: *ʾEino ḥai le-ʿolam.*

6. Num. 15:31.

7. The King James Version of the Bible reads: "That soul shall utterly be cut off."

8. *B. Sanhed.* 64b.

9. Hebrew: *Guf ugeviyya,* meaning perhaps "body"—inorganic, "bodily shape"—organic structure.

10. *B. Ber.* 17a. The whole text reads: "A favorite saying of Rav was, [our world is unlike the Hereafter], in the Hereafter there is no eating or drinking, no propagation or negotiations, no jealousy or hatred and no competition . . ." Rabinovitz, *Diqduqei Sofrim* to the above source, shows that the MSS do not have the passage "the world is not, etc,—*loʾ ke-ha-ʿolam ha-zeh ha-ʿolam ha-ba.*"

11. Cant. 3:11.

12. In that connection the Midrash has it that "the crown wherewith his mother crowned him . . . on the day of his wedding [means] the revelation of the Torah." Cf. *Mishnah Taʿanith,* IV, 8.

13. Isa. 51:11.

14. Hebrew: *She-yodeʿin u-massigin me-ʾamitat ha-qadosh barukh hu.*

15. 1 Sam. 25:29; *B. Ḥagigah* 12b; *Guide* I:41.

16. Ps. 31:19. "Oh how great is thy goodness, which thou hast laid up for them that fear thee; which thou hast wrought for them that trust in thee before the sons of men."

17. *M.T. Book of Knowledge, Yesodei Ha-Torah* 1:6.

18. Deut. 22:7.

19. Num. 31:1.

20. *M.T. Yesodei ha-Torah* 4:9, *Hilkhot Teshuvah* 8:3.

21. *B. Ber.* 17a.

22. *M.T. Hilkhot Teshuvah,* chap. 3.

23. Ibid., chap. 8, *Hassagot RAbaD.*

24. *B. Ketubot* 111b.

25. Hebrew: *yaʿamdu, ʿamd*—to stand up.

26. *B. Sanh.* 92a.

27. *M.T. Hilkhot Teshuvah* 8:4.

28. Ibid. 8:8, *Hassagot.*

29. *B. Rosh Hashanah* 31a, *Sanhed.* 97a.

30. *Guide* II:29.

31. A. Freimann, the editor of Maimonides' *Responsa,* p.xliv, asserts that most of the questions which the scholars of Lunel addressed to Maimonides correspond almost exactly to RAbaD's objections. Cf. *M.T. Book of Love, Hilkhot Zizit* 2:6.

32. H. Gross maintains that Maimonides did not know RAbaD's objections, otherwise he would have answered him. *MGWJ,* vol. 23 (1874), p. 21.

33. *M.T. Hilkhot Teshuvah* 3:6.

34. I could not find the source of the expression "the coming of the redeemer" (*bi'at ha-go'el*). See, for instance, J. Kassowsky, *Otzar,* s.v.

35. *B. Rosh Hashana* 17a. The text does not have *min ha-Torah* (derived from the Law) as the Mishnah of *Sanhedrin,* chap. 10 has.

36. Quotation from *B. Berakhot* 60b.

37. I would like to thank the Jewish National and University Library, Jerusalem, for making a film of this MS available to me. My attention was drawn to this manuscript by the kindness of Dr. E. Wiesenberg and Dr. L. Jacobs of London.

38. *Guide* I:40.

39. Corruption (*fasād*): The antithesis of generation (Pines).

40. The quotations from the *Guide* in this work are from the English translation of S. Pines.

41. Eccles. 12:7.

42. *Guide* I:42.

43. *I Sam.* 25:29.

44. *Guide* I:42.

45. Ibid.

46. Deut. 5:30.

47. Deut. 22:7.

48. *B. Berakhot* 18 a–b.

49. *Guide* I:42.

50. Deut. 30:15.

51. Ps. 68:5. The usual meaning of *'aravot,* is "desert," "plains."

52. *Guide* I:70.

53. Literally: the all (Pines).

54. *B. Hagigah* 12b.

55. *Guide* I:70.

56. *Guide* I:72, II:10.

57. *Guide* I:40.

58. *M.T. Yesodei Ha-Torah* 4, *Hilkhot Teshuvah* 8.

59. *Guide* III:27.

60. Deut. 6:2.

61. *Guide* III:27.

62. *M.T. Book of Judges, Hilkhot Melakhim* 12.

63. *Guide* III:54.

64. Jer. 9:22–23.

65. *Treatise* 16, 22.

66. *Guide* II:27.

67. *Treatise* 41, 42.

68. *Guide* II:17.

69. *Guide* II:29.

70. *B. Avodah Zarah* 54b.

71. *Guide* II:29.

72. Ibid.

73. Ibid.

74. *Treatise* 37.

75. *Guide* II:29.

76. *Genesis Rabbah* 5.

77. *Guide* II:25.

78. *M.T. Book of Knowledge, Yesodei Ha-Torah* 10.

79. *M.T. Book of Judges, Hilkhot Melakhim* 11.

80. Moses ben Maimon, *Einleitung (Pereq Ḥeleq)* (ed. Holzer).

81. J. N. Epstein, *Mavo,* p. 1276, asserts that the copyists of the Commentary of Maimonides, originally written in Arabic, omitted the text of the Mishnah because other versions were used by Maimonides. R. Margaliot thinks that Maimonides used the version of the Cambridge MS of the Mishnah (ed. Lowe), *Sinai,* vol. 10 (1942), p. 185. In that MS, *Pereq Ḥeleq* begins with: "Those who have no share in the Hereafter." However, in the light of the Arabic text of the original MS of Maimonides' Commentary on the Mishnah, the facsimile of which was published by Edelman, we find the whole Mishnah, i.e.: "Every Jew possesses a share in the Hereafter, etc." The Arabic MS is now well known as Maimonides' autograph.

82. In the Cambridge MS R.8.26 (2) fol. 6, we have a different variant in the Hebrew translation: "but it is for the pious (*hasidim*) only."

83. It seems that another version of *Gen. Rabbah* is quoted since the printed text of *Gen. Rabbah* has a different version. *Gen. Rabbah* 13:4. It is more likely that the quotation is from the text of *B. Taʿanit* 7a. It would be interesting to point out that in the midrashic literature, resurrection of the dead is connected with the idea of dew (*ṭal*) and rain (*geshem*). Cf. *B. Ḥagigah* 12b, *B. Taʿanit* 7a, *Gen. Rabbah* 13:4, Mann, *Texts,* vol. 2, p. 1268, n. 631.

84. *B. Berakhot* 18 a–b.

85. At the end of his examination of the meaning and content of the *Thirteen Principles,* A. Hyman is of the opinion that "the resurrection of the dead is somewhat . . . difficult to harmonize with his [Maimonides'] general views. . . . Maimonides had to accept . . . some of the biblical miracles in a literal fashion." A. Hyman, "Maimonides' Thirteen Principles," p. 144.

86. *B. Sotah* 13b.

87. Moses ben Maimon, *Mishnah, Haqdamat Seder Zeraʿim,* p. 12.

2

The Treatise on the
Resurrection of the Dead
as a Pro-Maimonidean Composition

The text of the *Treatise on Resurrection*[1] is ascribed to Maimonides, not only because the opening sentences make this claim (in the Hebrew text only, which is thought to be a translation of Ibn Tibbon from the Arabic), but also because the *Treatise* itself is written as if Maimonides had intended to say that he, Moses ben Maimon, author of the well-known books, the *Commentary of the Mishnah,* the *Ḥibbur* (*Mishneh Torah*), and the *Guide of the Perplexed,* finds himself forced to write a special and detailed work on the subject of resurrection for those who misunderstood his views as given in his other works. However, in this special treatise he adds nothing to what he has already written. The *Treatise* is only a repetition and fuller explanation for the sake of the general public, so that even women would be able to understand it (*Treatise 21*). This is the reason for the apologetic attitude in the *Treatise.* We shall not go into the details of the linguistic problems of the *Treatise,* which have already been dealt with by J. Finkel, D. H. Baneth, and J. L. Teicher.[2] Our aim in this study is to show that the *Treatise on Resurrection* could not have been written by Maimonides, not only because of the confused and unusual style, which does not resemble the style of his other works, but also and mainly because of the content of the *Treatise* and of the deductions which may be drawn from it. In the first place, why should an author of the caliber of Maimonides write a long treatise on a subject with which he could have dealt elsewhere, e.g., in the *Book of Knowledge?* It could, of course, be argued against this that Maimonides changed his opinion on the question of resurrection *after* he had already completed his main works. We cannot accept this argument since it is unbelievable that such a serious subject as

31

resurrection escaped Maimonides' attention when he dealt with the
main tenets of the Jewish religion in the *Book of Knowledge*. Furthermore, if it were true that Maimonides did alter his opinion, why did
he not add his new ideas on the matter to the text of the *Book of
Knowledge*? As far as is known from Maimonides' method of writing,[3] he did not hesitate to add to, or even to change, the text, as he
did, for example, in *Mishneh Torah*. Another question that one
should bear in mind is why should Maimonides have written a long
treatise on a subject of belief, only for the sake of his reputation
(*Treatise* 2, 4, 26, 53)? For what purpose would Maimonides have
gone to all the trouble of writing a complicated treatise which has
many moot points that only add to its complications? Even assum-
ing that Maimonides wrote it, not for the Jewish public, but for the
scholars who questioned his belief in resurrection, it would be
impossible to escape the ambiguity of the content of the *Treatise,* the
gist of which is: Bodily resurrection will take place sometime in the
future, perhaps during the Messianic era, and a second death will
follow. The Hereafter, in which only the life of the soul exists, has
no connection with resurrection. The future reward and punishment
of the soul and body must be preceded by the miracle of resurrection. The internal contradiction of this theory in the *Treatise* could
have been presented only to a public that was interested in exactly
this sort of interpretation of future eschatological events. However,
Maimonides' personality and authority stood high above the need
to adapt himself to this type of popular need. The alternative, which
suggests that Maimonides wrote the *Treatise* for a wider public, can
hardly be accepted. The *Treatise* is much too complicated for laymen,
who, presumably, were not acquainted with the *Guide of the Perplexed,* which is referred to several times in the *Treatise,* or even with
the *Mishneh Torah,* copies of which were available, in Maimonides'
time, only at the centers of study in the Jewish communities.

The author of the *Treatise* makes every effort to copy Maimonides' way of expressing himself. He makes the point that Maimonides usually expresses himself concisely, therefore it would be
useless to "quote all the *derashot* and *haggadot* (the talmudic exegesis)
[in connection with the subject of resurrection] since one can read
them in their original text" (*Treatise* 37). By mentioning *derashot* and

haggadot, the author alludes to the Gemara of Tractate *Sanhedrin,* the main part of which is *Aggadah.* In spite of the author's intention to be brief, the *Treatise on Resurrection* is rather long and incorporates many repetitions. The following is a short summary of the text of the *Treatise.*

Paragraphs 1–4 begin with a general and apologetic introduction which explains that the author has been misunderstood by his readers. He had emphasized the subject of the Hereafter, and therefore some people doubted his position on the subject of resurrection. However, even the words of God have been wrongly interpreted. For example the verse "Hear, O Israel: The Lord our God is one Lord" has been mistakenly understood by the Christians as an indication of the doctrine of the Trinity, while the true intention was to emphasize the unity of God. Maimonides' intention in his halakhic works is educational, and those works that are designed for the wider public include the statutes of the "laws of the Torah" and the basic articles of faith.

Paragraphs 5–14 continue to survey Maimonides' works, the Introduction to the *Commentary of the Mishnah* of *Pereq Ḥeleq* and the *Mishneh Torah,* which also contain explanations of articles of faith. The belief in the Hereafter, and not the belief in resurrection, is the ultimate object *(takhlit aharon),* although resurrection is also an article of faith. For that reason he has discussed the subject of the Hereafter at length. In the Hereafter there is no corporeal existence, because God does not create anything unnecessarily. One should not cite the example of Moses or Elijah, whose bodies existed without food. The general public cannot grasp an abstraction.

Paragraphs 15–20 deal with the events which preceded the writing of the *Treatise.*

Paragraphs 21–30 (the major part of which is quoted in *Yad Ramah*) explain that the aim of the *Treatise* is to clarify the subject of resurrection, although there is nothing new in it in addition to what Maimonides has already said. Maimonides did not say that the resurrection which is alluded to in the Bible is a metaphor. The verses in Daniel should not be interpreted allegorically. Only the dead of Ezekiel belong to the category of allegory. Those who will be resurrected will live a long life and die again. The soul in the Hereafter lives an eternal life. It is impossible to deny resurrection because this means the denial of miracles. To deny miracles leads to the abandoning of faith. Nothing in Maimonides' writings teaches the denial of resurrection. He who asserts otherwise is misjudging his opinion. Some of the verses have an allegorical meaning, some are unclear, and only those in the Book of Daniel are to be understood literally. The latter verses give ample evidence on resurrection, the meaning of which is that the soul will return to the body. Those who suspect that Maimonides denies resurrection when he states that the Messiah is not expected to perform miracles are mistaken. His intention is to make clear that the performing of miracles will not be the measure by which the Messiah will have to prove himself as the Messiah.

Paragraphs 31–53 continue to deal with verses which have an allegorical meaning. Maimonides' method is to coordinate religion and reason, and to explain everything according to the laws of nature, as far as possible. Only that which cannot be explained otherwise must be a miracle. One should distinguish between miracles, which happen only at a given moment, and natural occurrences, which are continuous in accordance with the nature of the world. No proof can be adduced from miracles. Maimonides discusses at length the subject of the Hereafter and is very brief on the subject of resurrection. All his works are written to the point. He had to write at greater length on the Hereafter because it is an abstract subject, though it falls within the laws of nature, while resurrection is a miracle and thus a mere matter of belief. It is typical of Maimonides that he expresses himself concisely. But the *Treatise* is a repetition of opinions that have already been expressed in his other works—that is to say, it is not all concise. Nevertheless, two new points are added to the *Treatise:* How is it that many verses in the Torah deny resurrection, and how is it that resurrection is not mentioned? The answer to the first question is that the biblical verses deal with the laws of nature. It is in the nature of animals and men to perish. The souls of men remain, and this is also according to nature. This statement does not contradict the belief in the future resurrection of those whom God chooses.

Resurrection is a miracle. Belief in the creation of the world includes belief in miracles. The answer to the second question is that the subject of resurrection could not have been revealed at the time of the revelation of the Torah. The people who lived in those days were unable to grasp the meaning of resurrection. Only generations later, when the predictions of the prophets had been fulfilled, did the prophets tell of resurrection, and then it was easy to perceive. Its success or failure (*tiqun vehefsed*) does not depend on natural causes but on the ability of the Jewish people to obey the Law. Miracles can be divided into two categories, namely, those which occur in natural matters and those which occur in unnatural matters. The question why resurrection, which precedes the reward and punishment after death, is not a miracle, should not be asked. Everything depends on God's wisdom. The *Treatise* is a repetition for the general public, whereas scholars are content with a short explanation. One should express one's opinions in accordance with the perception of a given public.

Up to this point we have summarized the *Treatise on Resurrection*. We would now like to discuss some points of the *Treatise* which arise in the above summary.

It is interesting to notice that the verse "Hear, O Israel, etc." (*Shema͑ Israel*), which is mentioned in the *Guide of the Perplexed* only once,[4] and in a vague connotation, is used by the author of the *Treatise* to show that the Christians misinterpret the Bible, building on that verse their conception of the Trinity. In Judaism it is understood as the basis for the perception of the unity of God (*Treatise* 1). Maimonides refers to this verse when he explains the unity of God in *Mishneh Torah*.[5] The odd thing about the *Treatise* is that the author draws a comparison between the words of God that were wrongly understood by men, and the words of a human being, i.e., himself in this case, on the subject of the Hereafter (*Treatise* 2), which words were also misunderstood. Could Maimonides himself have used such extremely apologetic language? Is it, perhaps, that that opening of the *Treatise* is intended also to attract Christian readers, or at least those currents of thought in Judaism which tended to accept, by interpreting them in their own way, certain Christian views? The author of the *Treatise* uses the term *holei ha-nefashot* (those sick of soul) to indicate those who were unable to understand what he really meant.[6] Instead of getting straight to the point, the author explains again what has been misunderstood, probably for those "sick of soul," and goes into details about the true meaning of the works of Maimonides (*Treatise* 2, 3). He wants to convince the readers that it would be wrong to discuss the branches of religion (*se'ifei ha-dat*) without discussing its roots (*shorashim*). He means that the subject of resurrection belongs to the branches, whereas the subject of the Hereafter belongs to the roots. The *Treatise* refers several times to *Pereq Ḥeleq,* namely, the Introduction to Maimonides' *Commentary of the Mishnah* of that chapter, to *Mishneh Torah,* and to the *Guide*. Again and again the author returns to emphasize the root, the *'olam ha-ba* (the Hereafter), and leaves *teḥiyyat ha-metim* (resurrection) undefined because it is not the ultimate object (*Treatise* 8). The author's opinion on resurrection is expressed in a later part of the *Treatise,* which part is a direct result of the polemics of Maimonides' opinions. We have already shown (p. 15) that the only instance in which the term "resurrection of the dead" is mentioned in *Mishneh Torah* is really derived from the Talmud. The author of the *Treatise* alludes to that source in a very meticulous way: "In the *Ḥibbur* we also counted those who have no share in the Hereafter, and we included them in a definite number, namely, [exactly] the number twenty-four, because we were afraid that one of the copyists might miss an item out of the lot, and somebody might say that we did not mention it. And to those twenty-four that we counted belongs also he who denies resurrection of the dead" (*Treatise* 8). This seems to be a very complicated explanation which does not add much clarity to the subject itself. It is true that he who denies resurrection appears among the twenty-four who have no share in the Hereafter. But that is all. Whereas most of the twenty-four categories of deniers are gone into more fully in *Mishneh Torah,*[7] resurrection is not only not explained further, but not even referred to again.

The author of the *Treatise* explains resurrection as a miraculous phenomenon (*Treatise* 27, 37). He asserts that the "denial of miracles means the denial of a basic article of faith (*kefirah ba-'iqqar*) and the abandoning of religion (*Treatise* 27). Therefore we consider resurrection of the dead as a cornerstone of the Law (*mipinot ha-Torah*), and there is nothing at all in our writings (*devareinu*) which teaches the denial of the return of the soul to the body, but only the contrary, namely, that the soul returns to the body." If the above statement comes from Maimonides, how can we explain that in the *Book of Knowledge* Maimonides uses the term "denial of a basic article of faith" (*kafar ba-ʿiqqar*) to mean "denial of the existence of God," "on which everything else depends,"[8] whereas here, in the *Treatise,* the author asserts that belief in miracles is a basic article of faith and the denial of this article of faith is *kefirah ba-ʿiqqar.* Maimonides does not interchange his terms indiscriminately.

This seems to be a contradiction between Maimonides in *Mishneh Torah* and the author of the *Treatise.* Traces of a polemical discussion can be distinguished in the following passage: "He who prefers . . . to attribute to us an opinion which we do not hold . . . and to explain our writings by a farfetched explanation," meaning that Maimonides stated that the soul will *never* return to the body, "will be condemned" (*Treatise* 27). The real justification for the composition of the *Treatise* comes up only after the author has already written the major part of it. He admits that there are only two new topics in the *Treatise* which are not dealt with in the other works of Maimonides, namely, the meaning of many biblical verses which explicitly reject the idea of the resurrection of the dead, with the exception of the verse in Daniel which led to confusion among those who tried to explain its meaning (*Treatise* 38), and the question why the subject of resurrection is not even hinted at in the Law (*Treatise* 39). It is notable that these very two topics are not quoted in the *Dissertation* in Meir Abulafia's book *Yad Ramah,* as we shall see later on.

The author explains that it is customary for the Bible to record events that happen in accordance with the usual course of nature. Death is, indeed, a natural event, and although it is "beyond nature that man, once dead, should after his death return to life again . . . it is, however, man alone who is the recipient of divine emanation, and he alone possesses something that will not perish. . . . His body will perish and this is in accordance with nature."[9] But "resurrection itself belongs to [the category] of miracles" (*Treatise* 40–41). Such is the answer in the *Treatise* to the query why the verses reject resurrection, and the point that resurrection is a miracle is stressed again. As to the other query, why resurrection was not mentioned in the Pentateuch, the author explains that this topic could not have been revealed to the Jewish people before they had accepted as true the prophecy and the occurrence of miracles (*Treatise* 47). Both answers do not fit Maimonides' opinion in the *Guide of the Perplexed*. Maimonides believes in miracles which took place as recounted in the Bible, and lasted for a short time only, and this excludes resurrection (p. 25). The other answer, too, does not express the idea which is deduced from Maimonides' concept in the *Guide*. The *Treatise* develops the idea of progress in the belief in miracles, whereas Maimonides, in the *Guide,* develops his concept of the law of progress in the evolution that occurs in the ideas of human society. Maimonides bases this concept on the biblical verse that explains why "God led them (the people of Israel) not through the way of the land of the Philistines, although it was near . . . but . . . through the wilderness of the Red Sea . . ."[10] That is to say, that a long period (from the human point of view) was needed in order to prepare the Israelites for their entrance into the land of promise. The same applies to progress which occurs in the evolution of ideas and of morals in human society.[11] On the other hand, the author of the *Treatise* uses the same verse in order to explain the meaning of progress in the belief in the miracle of resurrection. That is, the verse, and the explanation which Maimonides used to develop the idea of progress in the morals of society, is used by the author of the *Treatise* to explain the idea of resurrection.

In the last part of the *Treatise,* a hypothetical question arises (*Treatise* 52): "He who asks why that miracle (which is mentioned in the Bible) was introduced to them instead of introducing the ultimate object as a miracle,[12] namely, the resurrection of the dead, and reward and punishment of the *body* and the *soul after death,* resembles the question which asks why the miracles [performed] by the messenger of God were what they were, as [for instance], the changing of the stick into a serpent, and not the changing of a stone into a lion." The answer to this hypothetical question is that everything depends on God's wisdom, which is beyond human understanding. The formal structure of the question is similar to the question asked by Maimonides in the *Guide* about the problem of miracles: "Why did He privilege the prophet with those particular miracles and not with others? What was God's aim in giving this Law? . . . The answer to all these questions [is]: He wanted it this way; or, His wisdom required it this way."[13] The above-quoted passage of the *Treatise* gives an entirely new meaning to the terms "reward," "punishment," "Hereafter," and "resurrection of the dead," which terms become combined with the term "miracle." When we examine the sentence ". . . why that miracle was introduced to them instead of introducing the ultimate object as a miracle, namely, the resurrection of the dead and reward and punishment of the *body* and the *soul after death*," we must come to the conclusion that at this point a new theory of the whole matter comes up, a theory that contradicts the whole previous argument of the *Treatise*. The author of the *Treatise* holds that although a physical resurrection, which should be regarded as a miracle, will take place sometime in the future, it is the Hereafter which is the *ultimate object,* i.e., the raison d'etre for the existence of a human being (*Treatise* 24). The author quotes from Maimonides' statement in *Mishneh Torah* about the absence of bodies in the life of the Hereafter. He explains in detail why the existence of bodies in the Hereafter is meaningless. Suddenly, resurrection of the dead has become the ultimate object, instead of the spiritual Hereafter, and resurrection is now connected with reward and punishment after death, which is an important concept of the Christian religion. The sentence ". . . why . . . instead of introducing the ultimate object as a miracle, meaning the resurrection of the dead and reward and punishment of the body and the soul after death" is in sharp contradiction to the previous part of the *Treatise,* where the author accepts Maimonides' view about the purely spiritual life of the Hereafter. The author imitates the language of the *Guide* when he asks the hypothetical question about resurrection, and copies the answer of the *Guide.* Thus he shows that in his opinion, the real meaning of the ultimate object is bodily resurrection and reward and punishment of the body and soul after death. That conclusion is inserted in the *Treatise* in an unobtrusive way, and changes the whole meaning of the previous exposition of the *Treatise.* The following deduction is obvious: Maimonides could not have made such a statement, which opposes his teachings and attitude to the subjects of resurrection and the Hereafter. Only someone who wishes to convince his readers that Maimonides did indeed believe in bodily resurrection and in a corporeal reward and punishment after death, could have composed a complicated discussion which combines Maimonidean views with other views which have been twisted into the original texts of Maimonides.

Up to now, we have discussed some of the main problems with which the *Treatise on Resurrection* deals. In our examination of the text of *Yad Ramah,* we shall analyze some other passages of the *Treatise* which are quoted in that text. In conclusion, we see that although the author of the *Treatise* keeps repeating that he really does not add anything new to the opinions which are already expressed in Maimonides' writings, most of the "additions" flatly contradict the said writings. It would be difficult to accept that Maimonides, after having expressed his opinions in his main works, was compelled, under a certain external pressure of public opinion, to change his point of view about the resurrection of the dead. For whom would Maimonides have written a complicated treatise with the declared aim of clearing his reputation by stating that the "soul returns to the body after death" (*Treatise* 21) and that this is to be regarded as a miracle (*Treatise* 37)? He could surely have found a simpler and clearer way to express himself on this point. It seems that someone who was very well versed in Maimonides' writings, and who wished to emphasize the belief of Maimonides in physical resurrection, took upon himself (or it could have been a group of pro-Maimonideans) the composition of an intricate treatise on the subject of resurrection, and used every possible device to convince the reader that it was written by Maimonides.

In the source material which we have, there is no mention of an extra treatise on resurrection written by Maimonides. The texts which include material on the controversy about Maimonides' belief in resurrection, and seem to be the nearest, chronologically, to Maimonides' time, would probably have included some traces of the *Treatise* if the authors of these texts had known it. On the contrary, two of these texts are reflected in the *Treatise* itself, a fact which suggests that the author of the *Treatise* already knew about the controversy.

We would like to outline here the first phase of the polemics on

Maimonides' opinion about the "Hereafter," since, as it seems, these polemics found an answer in the *Treatise on Resurrection*.

1. It began with Maimonides' explicit denial of corporeal resurrection in *Mishneh Torah*.

2. RAbaD, Maimonides' contemporary, objects to Maimonides' statement. This is the *first* reaction to Maimonides' denial of resurrection, and is not mentioned in any of the other texts which belong to the first phase of the polemics.

3. It is probable that Maimonides never learned of RAbaD's objection because there is no written reply.

4. Rabbi Meir ha-Levi Abulafia of Toledo attacks the same Maimonidean text. He turned to the scholars of Lunel for support of his attack against Maimonides and got an answer from them, refuting his arguments. Abulafia wrote again to Lunel. It seems that at least a part of the correspondence took place at the end of Maimonides' life (ca. 1200).

5. Sheshet, the *nasi* (head of the Jewish community), writes a sharp letter to Lunel against Abulafia's attack on Maimonides.

6. Some of the allegations made by Abulafia and Sheshet appear in the *Treatise on Resurrection*.

7. Abulafia's first letter to Lunel and the answer to it, Abulafia's second letter to Lunel, and Sheshet's letter are all part of the polemic which represents various currents of religious thought prevailing in Judaism in the first half of the thirteenth century. The nucleus of the polemic was Maimonides' attitude in *Mishneh Torah* toward the subject of the Hereafter.

8. The book *Yad Ramah* includes a separate *Dissertation* which develops the ideas that are expressed in the various texts of the

polemics and adds a new aspect to the meaning of the *Treatise on Resurrection*.

9. The *Treatise on Resurrection* includes the components of inner-Jewish polemics fused with a version of the Christian meaning of resurrection.

The preceding list gives us several external sources which, together, illuminate the first phase of the polemics about Maimonides' opinion on the Hereafter. Two of these external sources to which we refer as having been alluded to in the *Treatise* are the letters of Meir ha-Levi Abulafia and Sheshet *nasi* of Saragossa to Lunel.[14] Both letters deal with Maimonides' opinion on the Hereafter. Maimonides states in *Mishneh Torah* that bodies do not exist in ʿolam haba. This statement is quoted in the *Treatise* and is followed by the comment that it is absurd to think that God would create anything in vain; as, for example, bodies and organs in the Hereafter, where they are of no avail (*Treatise* 9). At this point an echo of the controversy about Maimonides' statement is heard. The author of the *Treatise* uses the arguments which are expressed in the letters of Abulafia and Sheshet. Abulafia maintains in his letter[15] that bodies exist in the Hereafter and that this existence must be preceded by bodily resurrection. Abulafia starts his argument by asking how a body could exist without food. The same question, which probably belongs to the controversy about Maimonides' opinion, is raised in the *Treatise* and in Sheshet's letter. Abulafia answers that bodily existence without food is possible because Moses and Elijah existed so. The author of the *Treatise* and Sheshet both reject this answer on the grounds that the cases of Moses and Elijah are no proof of conditions in the Hereafter. The *Treatise* maintains that their existence without food cannot be compared to the eternal life in the Hereafter (*Treatise* 10), and Sheshet maintains[16] that the cases of Moses and Elijah belong to an exceptional situation, a miracle. They also assert that the bodies of Moses and Elijah were not kept alive in vain because they returned to ordinary life. The author of the *Treatise* opposes Abulafia's opinion that the resurrected will live an eternal life, and makes a compromise between that opinion and Maimonides' opinion by asserting that resurrection will take place, but that the resurrected will die again. Sheshet, on the other hand, completely rejects a possible future resurrection. He admits himself unable to deny the verity of the miracles of the past, including resurrection. Sheshet is a true disciple of Maimonides. He explains that to maintain that the wisdom and knowledge of God are subject to change in the same way as the wisdom and knowledge of men is to deny a basic article of faith (*kafar ba-ʿiqqar*).[17] He believes that God, during the process of the creation of the world, created everything, and that no change will occur during the natural course of the world. The miracles that have happened—for example, the dividing of the sea and resurrection—were only temporary. The explanation of the past phenomenon of resurrection is, according to Sheshet, that this phenomenon should be considered a miracle.

It seems that that theory is developed in the *Treatise* under the influence of the letter of Sheshet and is used by the author of the *Treatise* to uphold his own theory, namely, that a future miracle of resurrection will occur, an explanation which is alien to the Maimonidean point of view. Sheshet mentions in his letter (we deal with a part of it on p. 99) the name "Meir," probably Meir Abulafia, whom he calls "a proud youth" who dared to attack Rabbi Moshe (Maimonides)[18] by writing a letter to Rabbi Jonathan (of Lunel)[19] and accusing Maimonides of the denial of resurrection of the dead.[20] Sheshet refers to the *Book of Knowledge* and accepts it as the highest authority. He claims that Meir was unable to understand Maimonides' work, although all Maimonides' opinions are proved to be right. Sheshet rejects all the proofs that Meir Abulafia brought in his letter and shows how ridiculous they are. It seems that the letter of Sheshet, which was a reaction to Abulafia's letter, was written during the lifetime of Maimonides, perhaps between the years 1200 and 1204. That Meir Abulafia was a young man when he wrote to Lunel is evident from the reply he received from the Lunel scholars. Neither the letter of Abulafia nor the letter of Sheshet mention a treatise on resurrection of possible Maimonidean authorship. Sheshet is well acquainted with the *Mishneh Torah* of Maimonides, which he mentions, and it is almost certain that he knew the *Guide of the Perplexed,* a book which he does not mention.

He is also well read in various Arabic books on philosophy, from which he adduces proof of the meaning of the term "resurrection of the dead." It may be that Sheshet does not mention the *Guide,* although he makes use of its arguments, because at that stage, as it is made clear from the Abulafia-Lunel correspondence, the controversy was based on Maimonides' halakhic and *not* philosophic ideas. Sheshet adapts Maimonidean views to his own explanation of miracles.[21] Miracles took place in answer to the need of the moment (*lezorekh hasha'ah*) and were of temporary duration only. The example which he brings is "the dividing of the sea and the resurrection of the dead."[22] Sheshet gives the term "resurrection of the dead" a precise interpretation. He claims that it refers to *the immortality of the soul:*[23] "[This is] the reward for the righteous in the future." Sheshet explains that "this is generally accepted. Most philosophers, who are theologians (*hakhamim ʾelohiyyim*), maintain that the intellect (*hanefesh hamaskelet*) that returns to its Creator . . . lives an eternal life (*hayah hayyei ʿolam*), and this is really [the meaning] of the term 'resurrection of the dead.' If you find some among those who pretend to be scholars, or [even] among the scholars or even among our true talmudic scholars, who maintain that the resurrection of the dead means the return of the soul to the body, and that a corporeal paradise exists . . . you must know that they have said so only for the sake of fools who are unable to understand . . ."[24]

Sheshet is of the opinion that the prophecies of "all the prophets have a metaphorical meaning" only.[25] This applies also to Ezekiel's prophecy about the resurrection of the dry bones. Sheshet, however, is bound to acknowledge that a resurrection of the dead has taken place in the past. The resurrection in the past was a temporary miracle, and as such it meant the *return of the soul to the body.* The return of the soul to the body is only implied by Sheshet. The author of the *Treatise* adapted Sheshet's idea that bodily resurrection was a miracle. He admits that such a resurrection will occur in the future, which idea is a compromise between two extreme views—that is to say, Maimonides' implicit denial of bodily resurrection in *Mishneh Torah,* and the explicit belief of RAbaD and Abulafia that the resurrection will not be followed by death. The *Treatise* wants the reader to understand that although Maimonides states that in the

Hereafter only a spiritual life of the soul exists, he nevertheless maintains that corporeal resurrection will take place, but this fact is not connected with the Hereafter. This will be a miracle, but not a temporary miracle, because the purpose of resurrection is, according to the last passages of the *Treatise,* the ultimate object, which precedes the last judgment before the reward and punishment of the body and the soul after death. This concept contradicts the first statement of the *Treatise,* where it is made clear that the resurrected will die again. Sheshet is a pro-Maimonidean who understands the meaning of the opinions which Maimonides expressed in *Mishneh Torah* as a halakhist and a philosopher, and he fights for these opinions as well as for Maimonides' reputation.

The author of the *Treatise* is also a pro-Maimonidean, but he stands very far from the true concept of Maimonides' teaching. His aim is undoubtedly to clear Maimonides' reputation, working in an opposite direction to that of Sheshet by putting into Maimonides' mouth not only opinions which he did not express, but also opinions which are entirely alien to his way of thinking. The traces of the external sources of the polemics in the *Treatise,* such as the letters of Abulafia and Sheshet, show that the *Treatise* was written at a period when the polemics had already been going on for some time. Our conclusion is that the *Treatise on Resurrection* was not originally written by Maimonides. The main reason for the composition of the *Treatise* was to create the impression that Maimonides truly believed in a future return of the soul to the body, which belief is an important Christian doctrine.[26]

One of the most outstanding facts about the *Treatise* is that the known sources which deal with the polemics about Maimonides' opinion on the Hereafter do not mention the existence of the *Treatise.*[27] The necessity for an apologetic statement was probably rather urgent. This fact throws light on the social position of the Jewish communities in France which led to the burning of Maimonides' books. The Jews had to vindicate Maimonides of heresy, that is to say, from disbelief in resurrection. This was the task of the *Treatise.* The following texts, in which the polemics are reflected, maintain that Maimonides' opinions on the Hereafter in *Mishneh Torah* were the immediate cause of the controversy.

These texts, which do not mention the *Treatise,* are:

1. *Kitāb-al-rasā'il,* which includes the correspondence between Rabbi Meir Abulafia of Toledo and the Jewish scholars of Lunel and their answers.[28]

2. The epistle of Sheshet *nasi* of Saragossa. Both sources are dealt with in the above discussion.

3. Yarḥi's commentary on *Kallah Rabbati,*[29] a main part of which deals with the polemics. The commentary is a secondary source; its author sums up the correspondence which is included in *Kitāb-al-rasā'il* and quotes a part of the reply of Rabbi Samson of Sens to Abulafia.[30] The text of Yarḥi does not contain a personal view on the controversy. It also includes a similar midrashic interpretation which appears in the book *'Arugat ha-Bosem.*[31]

4. Abraham ben ʿAzriel's *'Arugat ha-Bosem,* written about 1234,[32] is an important source for Hebrew literature of the Middle Ages in Germany and France, mainly for liturgical material. Some aspects of the polemics are intermingled in several passages of *'Arugat ha-Bosem* which deal with resurrection, the Hereafter, and the Messianic era.[33] The *Treatise* is unknown to Abraham ben Azriel. The author of *'Arugat ha-Bosem* was familiar with the letter by Meir Abulafia, but he was not aware of the *Dissertation* in *Yad Ramah,* which includes a long quotation from the *Treatise* (p. 107). The above-mentioned facts would change the date of the composition of the *Treatise* from the beginning of the last decade of the twelth century to the last decade of the first half of the thirteenth century.[34]

5. *Milḥamot hashem-* written by Abraham, the son of Maimonides, in answer to the burning of Maimonides' books in France (ca. 1234). This text, too, does not mention the *Treatise.*[35] Abraham discusses at length the meaning of the Hereafter as understood by his father. Had there been any change in those opinions, it would undoubtedly have been reflected in his discussion.

6. Cambridge MS. Add. 507. 1., which is an incomplete manu-script[36] of a letter addressed to some French Rabbis. According to that letter, the Rabbis joined the leader of the anti-Mai-monidean group in Montpellier, Solomon min-hahar and his disciples, Jonah Ghirondi, and David ben Saul, in their ban on the *Book of Knowledge* and the *Guide of the Perplexed*. The above letter was probably written in France[37] during the lifetime of Rabbi David Kimḥi[38] (d. 1235), who took part in the polemics as a pro-Maimonidean.[39] The writer warns those who banned Mai-monides' works to change their attitude because the authorities might exploit the inner religious conflict of the Jewish commu-nity for their own aims: *"Pen yomru ha-moshlim ʿaleikhem poshim ʾatem ʿal shtei ha-seʿippim vi-yer ʾetem le-nafshoteikhem meʿasot zot."*[40] In an earlier passage of the MS, the writer says: "We also believe in the resurrection of the dead, that is to say, that God will return souls to their bodies, which is according to the tradition which has come down to us from the Torah literally (*kifshuṭo*). [The resurrection of the dead] is a miracle, that is to say that God will change the course of nature (*minhag ha-ʿolam*) for his pious adherents . . ."[41] This confession of faith reminds us of the *Treatise,* which is not mentioned in the MS.

While the above-mentioned texts do not know anything about the *Treatise on Resurrection,* there are some texts attributed to Maimonides which allude to a composition that might be the treatise under dis-cussion. However, after having come to a conclusion that the *Treatise* is not by Maimonides' pen, these texts, which include Responsa and some personal letters of Maimonides, must be care-fully examined, because they cannot be accepted as genuine in con-nection with the matter of resurrection. We refer to the following texts:

1. Maimonides' letter to Joseph ben Judah.[42]

2. Maimonides' response to Samuel ben Ali of Baghdad.[43]

3. Maimonides' letter to Joseph ibn Gabar, Baghdad;[44] Mai-

monides' letter to Ḥisdai, Alexandria.[45] The first letter is analyzed by J. L. Teicher in a detailed and systematic examination.[46] J. L. Teicher compares, step by step, the letter to Joseph ben Judah with the *Treatise on Resurrection,* and shows that the letter depends on the *Treatise.* The arguments of J. L. Teicher solve some chronological problems as well as some other difficult problems arising from the letter. The Responsa under consideration deal with the problem of traveling on big rivers on the Sabbath. Although the opinions of Samuel ben Ali and Maimonides differ on this question, it is evident that Samuel ben Ali was *not* an antagonist of Maimonides,[47] although he is described as such in the *Treatise* (par. 17). Some lines on the subject of resurrection appear in the above-mentioned response of Maimonides. Maimonides mentions there that he has already written a treatise on that subject (resurrection) in order to vindicate himself in that matter. This statement cannot be accepted as genuine. It was added to the response of Maimonides, probably from the same source of information that the author of the *Treatise* used. This information was undoubtedly used also by the author of the *Dissertation* in *Yad Ramah*[48] in the passage that describes the events which preceded the composition of the *Treatise.* It is also worth pointing out that Maimonides' reference to the *Treatise* appears only in an expanded manuscript and not in other parallel MSS. The response under consideration evidently contains interpolated material.[49] Whereas the letter to Joseph ben Judah furnishes the reader with the information that Maimonides intends to write a treatise on resurrection, the response furnishes the reader with information about a treatise already written by Maimonides. These statements are two sides of the same coin, namely, that the intention of the author was to add another proof to the authenticity of the *Treatise* itself. The conclusions which may be drawn from sources other than the *Treatise,* sources which are a part of the whole trend of clearing Maimonides' attitude toward corporeal resurrection, merely complicate further problems of the *Treatise.* The *Treatise still remains the main source* for the facts that are recorded in it. We would like to mention also that in another letter which is ascribed to Maimonides, the letter to Joseph ibn Gabar, it is stated that Maimonides has already written a treatise on resurrection which will probably reach the community of Baghdad. This is another parallel source to the statement which is given in the letter to Joseph ben Judah. The same applies to Maimonides' response to Rabbi Ḥisdai ha-Levi of Alexandria, which touches upon various theological questions. A passage in that response about resurrection explains that Maimonides holds that resurrection belongs to the category of miracles which are in contrast to nature. That assertation is similar to those made on the subject of miracles in the *Treatise* (pars. 32, 34, 37); nevertheless, the continuation of the response shows that Maimonides opposes anything which is not according to nature. We shall not discuss the two above-mentioned sources in this connection.

In conclusion, whatever the results of a thorough examination of all the letters and the *Responsa* might be, it is obvious that the passages which deal directly with resurrection belong to a certain stage in the polemics on Maimonides' opinion of the Hereafter. These passages were written in order to furnish complete support for Maimonides' authorship of the *Treatise*. On the other hand, it seems that some particulars of the data which are transmitted in the *Treatise,* in the letters and the *Responsa,* and in the *Dissertation* in *Yad Ramah,* are probably of the same origin and could be considered per se as genuine. We believe that Maimonides could not have written a treatise on resurrection because of his own point of view, but this conclusion does not necessarily exclude any objections that arose in connection with Maimonides' position, as for instance the objection of RAbaD. The *Treatise* furnishes us with some data as to the cause for its composition. RAbaD's objection is not mentioned in the *Treatise*. Other objections voiced by Eastern Jewry we know of only through the *Treatise* itself. It seems that there is no direct connection between the objection voiced in the Jewish community in the south of France and the objections which were probably expressed among the Jews of the Yemen and Damascus. The last-named country and city appear in the *Treatise,* while Lunel and Montpellier are unnamed, being mere echoes of the correspondence with regard to the polemics.

In addition to the polemics on Maimonides' position on the Hereafter or the resurrection, there is an Arabic text, a fragment of which is kept in the Library of Leningrad. Only some parts of this fragment have been published,[50] and therefore we are unable to get a true perspective of the meaning of this text. A. Harkavy, who edited these parts, suggests that the anonymous text should be considered as a tract which opposes another text of whose existence we learn only from our *Treatise,* since our *Treatise* attacks a certain text which is probably the same that is attacked in the Leningrad fragment. That is to say, the Leningrad fragment does in a certain way resemble the *Treatise,* and as such it must have been written against Samuel ben Ali, the Gaon of Baghdad, whose eschatological views are revealed and criticized in the *Treatise (Treatise* 17–20). J. L. Teicher, who calls this Arabic fragment the "Leningrad Tract," and calls the text which is alluded to in the *Treatise* the "Baghdad Pamphlet,"[51] comes to the conclusion that the Leningrad Tract is the source for the information which the author of the *Treatise* has about the Baghdad Pamphlet. J. L. Teicher sees in the Tract one of the sources that were used by the author of the *Treatise,* and not just a counterpart of the *Treatise.* The edited parts of the Leningrad fragment do not mention the name of Samuel ben Ali,[52] nor do they mention Maimonides. However, it is possible to identify these personalities after a close comparison between both texts, a comparison to which J. L. Teicher draws our attention in his study of the above texts.[53] As far as the *Dissertation* in *Yad Ramah* is concerned, it seems that the author of the *Dissertation* learned about the geographical details, as well as the names of the personalities, from the same text as did the author of the *Treatise* (p. 103). May we suppose that the author of the *Treatise* and the author of the *Dissertation* drew their information from the full text, a fragment of which is preserved in Leningrad?

Our discussion on the *Treatise on Resurrection* leads us to the conclusion that although the *Treatise* expresses some of Maimonides' original views about the Hereafter, quotes from his *Commentary of the Mishnah,* and mentions his philosophical work, it cannot be ascribed to Maimonides in the light of the proofs we have adduced. The *Treatise* is a pro-Maimonidean composition the aim of which was to convince the Jewish public (who were spiritually prepared for it), and through this public, the Christian authorities, that Maimonides believed in bodily resurrection.

There is only one external source, to our knowledge, which includes a long, important, and direct quotation from the *Treatise on Resurrection,* namely, the *Dissertation* on the subject of the Hereafter in the Book *Yad Ramah,* commonly ascribed to Meir ha-Levi Abulafia. In the next chapter we shall edit the whole text of the *Dissertation,* which comprises, in our opinion, the main source for understanding the *Treatise* itself, as well as the other texts about the controversy, and is the key to the solution of the question as to whether the *Treatise on Resurrection (Ma'amar Tehiyyat ha-Metim)* is by Maimonides.

Notes

1. Moses ben Maimon, *Ma'amar Tehiyyat ha-Metim* (ed. J. Finkel).

2. J. Finkel in his edition; D. H. Baneth, *Tarbiz,* vol. 11 (1940) and vol. 13 (1942); J. L. Teicher, *Melilah,* vol. 1 (1944), pp. 88 ff. Z. Graetz asserts that the *Treatise* was written in "a very strict orthodox spirit, which differs very much from that in all [Maimonides'] previous books and treatises." *Divrei,* vol. 5, p. 398.

3. Moses ben Maimon, *Responsa,* no. 240: "What we have written in the *Hibbur* is right . . . and so is what we have written in the Commentary of the Mishnah, and what you have found in the Commentary of the Mishnah, which is the opposite to what we had written in the *Hibbur,* is the *first edition* . . . but later we revised our opinion *(diqdaqnu bi-dvarenu)* etc."; no. 318: "We have added a certain explanation in the *Hibbur* for your sake . . ." See also nos. 306, 440, 453; *Guide* I, p. 10; S. K. Mirsky, *HaRaMbaM,* p. 78; Y. Kafaḥ, *Hazofe,* 20.12.68.

4. *Guide* III:45.

5. M.T. *Yesodei ha-Torah* 1:7.

6. The Arabic expression for *holei ha-nefashot, al-marḍā al-anfus,* means: "holding opinions that deviate from what is right." Lane, *Lexicon,* s.v. *mrḍ.*

7. M.T. *Book of Knowledge, Hilkhot Teshuvah* 3:14.

8. Ibid., *Hilkhot Yesodei Torah* 1:6.

9. Cf. *Guide* I:40.

10. Exod. 13:17.

11. J. L. Teicher, *Melilah,* vol. 1, (1944), p. 87.

12. In the Bodleian, Oxford MS (no. 2493³ in Neubauer Catalogue) of the *Treatise,* fol. 134, the version is: An important miracle *(mofet gadol).*

13. *Guide* II:25.

14. Abulafia, *Kitāb;* Sheshet, *Nusaḥ ha-Iggeret.*

15. Abulafia, *Kitāb,* p. 14.

16. Sheshet, *Nusaḥ ha-Iggeret,* p. 426.

17. Ibid., p. 420.

18. Ibid., p. 414.

19. Ibid, p. 415.

20. Ibid., p. 416.

21. Ibid., p. 420.

22. See also, *M.T. Yesodei ha-Torah* 10, *Hilkhot Melakhim* 11.

23. Sheshet, *Nusaḥ ha-iggeret,* p. 422.

24. Ibid., p. 425.

25. Ibid., p. 426.

26. W. Marxsen, *The Resurrection of Jesus,* p. 13. This study has a very interesting new outlook on the whole problem from the Christian point of view.

27. J. L. Teicher, *Melilah,* p. 82.

28. D. Yellin remarks that from a unique Arabic MS, Jerusalem, Hebr. 8, 61, it can be deduced that Abulafia wrote the preface to *Kitāb-al-rasāʾil* in Arabic, *Kirjath Sepher,* vol. 6 (1929), 139–144. However, the structure of *Kitāb-al-rasāʾil* should be reexamined.

29. Abraham ha-Yarḥi, *Commentary,* p. 342.

30. Ibid.

31. Ibid., p. 345.

32. The letter of Meir Abulafia to Lunel is mentioned in *ʿArugat ha-Bosem,* vol. 2, p. 259. According to E. E. Urbach, the author of *ʿArugat ha-Bosem* was the first to make use of all the parts of *Mishneh Torah.* E. E. Urbach asserts that the letter of Meir Abulafia, which touches, apart from the aspect of resurrection, upon some other halakhic subjects of Maimonides' *Mishneh Torah,* introduced *Mishneh Torah* to the communities of Northern France and Germany. *ʿArugat ha-Bosem,* vol. 4, p. 178; E. E. Urbach, *Zion,* vol. 12, p. 150. It seems, however, according to Maimonides' *Responsa,* that the scholars of Lunel had become acquainted with *Mishneh Torah* as soon as copies of that work reached them about 1180. It should also be pointed out that the above mentioned letter of Abulafia as quoted in *ʿArugat ha-Bosem* is quite different from the text in *Kitāb-al-rasāʾil.*

33. *ʿArugat ha-Bosem,* vol.1 pp. 256–268; vol. 4, p. 254.

34. M. Steinschneider, *Hebraeische Uebersetzungen,* p. 431; J. L. Teicher, *Melilah,* vol. 1 (1944), p. 92; idem, *JJS,* vol. 1, no. 1 (1948–49), p. 49, note 2.

35. Abraham ben Moses, *Milḥamot, Kovetz* III, pp. 17 ff., and the ed. of R. Margaliot.

36. This MS has been brought to my attention by Dr. Teicher. A part of the letter was published in *Kerem Ḥemed,* vol. 5 (1841), pp. 17ff. It is ascribed to Abraham ben Moses (Maimonides' son) by mistake. Z. Graetz, *Divrei,* vol. 5, ascribes the letter to Samuel Sasporta. The title of the Cambridge MS reads: ''אגרת שלוחה מאת הרב ר' אשר בר' גרשם על אדות מורה הנבוכים לרבני צרפת.'' J. Shatzmiller, who ascribes this letter

to Asher ben Gershom has thoroughly examined this manuscript. See his study in *Studies in the History of the Jewish People and the Land of Israel in Memory of Zvi Avnery* (Haifa, 1970), pp. 129–140 (Hebrew).

37. MS 507, fol. 69b.

38. Ibid., fol. 78b.

39. His letter to Rabbi Judah al-Fakhar is probably the earliest source which records the burning of Maimonides' books in Montpellier. See I. F. Baer, *History of the Jews in Christian Spain,* I, (1966), 400–401.

40. Cambridge MS 507. 1, fol. 74a.

41. Ibid., fol. 73a.

42. Moses ben Maimon, *Epistulae,* no. 6.

43. Idem, *Responsa,* ed. A. Freimann, nos. 68 and 69; ed. J. Blau, no. 310; *Kovetz,* I, no. 157.

44. *Kovetz,* II, p. 75.

45. Ibid., p. 23.

46. J. L. Teicher, *JJS,* vol. 1, no. 1 (1948–49) pp. 35–54.

47. S. Poznanski, *Babylonische Geonim,* p. 21 and p. 30.

48. *Yad Ramah* 14.

49. Vatican MS Neofiti ebr. 11.

50. A. Harkavy, *ZHB,* vol. 2, pp. 125–28, pp. 181–88. Our direct application to the University Library of Leningrad remained unanswered.

51. J. L. Teicher, *JJS,* vol. 1, no. 1 (1948–49), p. 43.

52. S. Poznanski asserts that in the Leningrad Tract, Samuel ben Ali is the person who appears as the opponent of Maimonides. *Babylonische Geonim,* p. 26.

53. J. L. Teicher, *JJS,* vol. 1, no. 1 (1948–49), pp. 43 ff.

3

An Edition and Translation of the Dissertation on Resurrection and Hereafter from the Hebrew Commentary on Pereq Ḥeleq in Yad Ramah*

Yad Ramah[1]
Pereq Ḥeleq[2]

1. Page 90 [Babylonian Talmud, Tractate *Sanhedrin* teaches]: "Every Jew possesses a share in the Hereafter, etc."[3] Thus we find in ancient and accurate texts where a point is made to adjoin *Pereq Ḥeleq*[4] to [chapter] *ʾelu hen ha-nisrafin*[5] whether in the texts of the Mishn[ah] or in the texts of the Gemar[a]. This is also [justified] because at the beginning [the Mishnah] lists [the categories] of those who should be executed (*neheragin*), which are given in the text *ʾelu hen ha-nisrafin,* as it is taught: "Those who should be executed: a murderer, the people of an apostate city." If you say that it is right that *Pereq Ḥeleq* should come after chapter *ʾelu hen ha-nisrafin* [then you are right] because [the Mishnah] having completed the subject of murderers, has yet to comment on the category: the people of an apostate city, who should be executed (*neheragin*), without which [its explanation] is incomplete, and which one would have expected to find in the chapter *ʾelu ha-nisrafin*. However, if you say that the [chapter] *ʾelu ha-nehnaqin*[6] precedes *Pereq Ḥeleq,* [then this is wrong] because the subject of those who should be executed (*ʾelu hen ha-neheragin*) has not

---

*The translation is specially adapted to the style of the Hebrew original. I tried to be faithful to its simplicity. Nevertheless, I had to add several words in square brackets—without which the literal translation would not have been sufficiently clear.

55

yet been exhausted, yet the [Mishnah is already] explaining chapter
nehnaqin. Therefore we must deduce that *pereq Heleq* precedes *'elu
ha-nehnaqin,* and both [*'elu hen ha-nehnaqin* and *Pereq Heleq*] are discussed at the end of *'elu hen ha-nisrafin.*[7] [And since the Mishnah goes
on to teach] that a layman who performs a function [in the Temple]
should be executed by divine intervention, the [Mishnah] continues
by expanding the category of those who [will be judged] by divine
intervention. [The Mishnah connects judgment by divine intervention (*bi-ydei shamayim*) with the Hereafter, and so from here it goes
on to teach]: "Every Jew possesses a share in the Hereafter."

2. [Here we start our explanation]: The subject of the Hereafter is a
fundamental article [of faith] in the Torah. [This premise must be
accepted] since he who denies it, even if he may have the knowledge
of the Torah and good deeds to his credit, he will have no share in
the Hereafter, as it is explicitly stated in the Mishn[ah][8] and further
clarified in the G[emara]. And, moreover, the justification of the
divine judgment depends on it (i.e., belief in the Hereafter),
namely, that "His eyes are open upon all the ways of the sons of
man; to give everyone according to his ways and according to the
fruit of his doings."[9] Therefore it is incumbent upon us to explain its
meaning [the meaning of the Hereafter] according to the tradition
that was handed down to us by our fathers and teachers, according
to the widespread tradition accepted by all Jews,[10] as well as according to the literal meaning of the Mishnah[11] and the oral traditions
(*shemu'ot*).[12] [We shall] not strive to perform extraordinary deeds or
search for great things, nor shall we question the tradition of our
fathers, nor make any innovations with our limited and mean intelligence, nor investigate the secrets that belong to the Lord our God.
The "what" and "why" of such matters are not of our concern.

3. The point about the Hereafter is that it is the period of time that
will follow several years after the Messianic era. The essential reward
for the righteous and the punishment of the wicked will take place
only *then,* as we are taught in *Avot:* "The world resembles a corridor
leading to the Hereafter. Make your preparations in the corridor so
that you may enter the dining-room in a proper state."[13] Hence, the

punishment of the wicked takes place only in the Hereafter, as is shown by the exegesis of biblical text in this chapter (of the Talmud):[14] "Cutting off (*hikkaret*); will be cut off (*tikkaret*).[15] *Hikkaret* [means] in this (physical) world, *tikkaret* [means] in the Hereafter."[16]

4. Although reward and punishment will both take place in the Hereafter, there are instances in which the term "Hereafter" is applied only to the reward [of the righteous], not to the punishment [of the wicked], as [for example] in the chapter: "Every Jew possesses a share in the Hereafter."[17] Likewise[18] the statement quoted above [from *Avot*][19]—"The world resembles a corridor leading to the Hereafter"—means that if you did not prepare yourself in the corridor, you will not enter the Hereafter. These statements refer only to the reward in the Hereafter, not to the punishment. Likewise, the statement in the Mishnah which follows—"The people of Sodom have no share in the Hereafter"[20] refers only to the reward in the Hereafter, not to the punishment. [It is so], since [in the text of the Mishnah] it is stated: "But they [the people of Sodom] will appear at the judgment."[21] There is no need to mention that whenever the term "life in the Hereafter" is used, it refers to reward alone.

5. The Hereafter [which is] referred to in our Mishnah is [to be understood] according to the literal meaning of the Mishnah[22] and the Talmud,[23] and also according to the widespread tradition accepted by all Jews[24] [as the time in which] both bodies and souls together, as they before their death, will appear[25] at the judgment. We have already written that the reward of the righteous and the punishment of the wicked will [take place] only in the Hereafter. Therefore it is impossible that [this could happen] without the body. This is proved from the text in the Gema[ra]:[26] "Antoninus said to Rabbi: 'The body and the soul can both free themselves from judgment. Thus[27] the body can plead: The soul has sinned, [the proof being] that from the day it left me I lie like a dumb stone in the grave [powerless to do aught]. Whilst the soul can say: The body has sinned, [the proof being] that from the day I departed from it I fly in the air like a bird [and commit no sin].' He [Rabbi] replied: 'I will tell thee a parable. To what can this be compared? To a human king

who owned a beautiful orchard which contained [91b] splendid figs.
Now, he appointed two watchmen therein, one lame and the other
blind. [One day] the lame man said to the blind: 'I see beautiful figs
in the orchard. Come and take me upon thy shoulder that we may
pick and eat them.' So the lame bestrode the blind, picked and ate
them. Sometime after, the owner of the orchard, came and inquired
of them, 'Where are those beautiful figs?' The lame man replied,
'Have I then feet to walk with?' The blind man replied, 'Have I then
eyes to see with?' What did he do? He placed the lame upon the
blind and judged them together. So will the Holy One, blessed be
He, bring the soul, [re]place it in the body, and judge them together,
as it is written, 'He shall call to the heavens from above and to the
earth, that he may judge his people.'[28] 'He shall call to the heavens
from above'—this refers to the soul; 'and to the earth, that he may
judge his people'—to the body.'' Another proof that the Day of
Judgment can take place only after the resurrection of the dead is
derived from the Mishnah: "He [Elazar Haqapar] used to say:
Those who are born will die, the dead will [become] alive, and the
living will be judged."[29] Hence you learn that after they are born
they die, and after their death they become alive, and after having
been alive (resurrected), they are judged.

The texts of the Mishnah and its Gemara are quite specific in
their teaching:[30] "Those who have no share in the Hereafter are: He
who maintains that there will be no resurrection [etc.]. It is asked in
the Gemara: "Why is it so? [Why is punishment so severe?]" And
the answer is: "Since all the qualities of God are based on the principle of exact compensation,[31] the person who denies resurrection of
the dead will therefore have no share in the resurrection of the
dead." Hence you have learned that the "Hereafter" mentioned in
our Mishnah is the resurrection of the dead.

And yet another point [about the Hereafter which we] learn from
the exegesis [in the talmudic text]:[32] "Whence is resurrection
[derived from the Torah], etc.? From the verse[33] 'cutting off' (hikkaret); 'will be cut off' (tikkaret).''[34] "Rabbi Joshua ben Levi said:
Whence is resurrection derived from the Torah? From the verse
'blessed are they that dwell in thy house: they shall ever praise thee,
Selah.'[35] The text does not have 'praised thee' but 'they shall praise

thee.'" Thus [we learn that] the resurrection [will take place in the future]. It also means that [the resurrection of the dead will happen] in the Hereafter, as Rabbi Joshua ben Levi himself said:[36] "Whoever uttereth a song [of praise to God] in this world shall be privileged to do so in the Hereafter, as it is said: 'They shall ever praise thee.'"[37] Hence you have learned that the resurrection of the dead will take place in the Hereafter.[38]

6. Yet another point derives from the text in *Berakhot:* "A favorite saying of Rav was: 'In the Hereafter there is no eating or drinking, no negotiations, no propagation, but the righteous sit with their crown[s] on their heads, and feast on the brightness of the divine presence.[39] If bodies are[40] [not] resurrected in the Hereafter, why did they need to say that all those things [eating, drinking] do not exist in it? They should have said that the body does not exist in it [in the Hereafter] and consequently all those [activities] would have automatically ceased. [That they do say so] is in order to tell you that although bodies exist in it, there is no eating or drinking. Therefore he (Rav) had to add: 'But the righteous sit with their crowns on their heads and feast on the brightness of the divine presence'[41] for if there are no bodily activities, from what will the righteous derive their enjoyment and what kind of reward will be theirs? To this, he answered: 'They sit with their crowns on their heads and feast on the brightness of the divine presence.'"

7. The following verses also show that the Day of Judgment makes no sense unless the resurrection of the dead [takes place]. As it is written: "And many of them that sleep in the dust of the earth shall awake, some to everlasting life and some to shame and everlasting contempt."[42] And it is written: "He shall call to the heavens from above and to the earth that He may judge his people."[43] Such is Rabbi's answer to Antoninus.[44] Thus, we have explained [our point, by relying on] the literal meaning of the [biblical] verse[s] and reinforcing it with the text of the Mishnah[45] and the oral traditions,[46] that the Hereafter, in which the righteous will be rewarded and the wicked punished, is inconceivable without a body. Such is also the widespread oral tradition of all Jews,[47] a teaching received by Moses

on Sinai (as part of the oral law, *Halakha le-Moshe mi-Sinai*). Our teacher, Saadiah [Gaon] of blessed memory, also expressed himself in the same [way] in his *Book of Beliefs*.[48] Also all the Geonim in their book[s] expressed themselves to the same effect.[49]

8. Reason also suggests that just as justice (*middat ha-din*) requires that the soul be rewarded for its integrity and punished for its trespasses, so justice requires that the body be rewarded for its integrity and punished for its trespasses, since both of them have done the deed, whether good or evil. If bodies are not resurrected, what hope can they have? Who can expect any hope for them? Who will compensate the body for its integrity and its trespasses? The body did it, who will give it the reward?[50]

9. If you raise the objection that the body is not judged because without the soul it would be like a stone which nobody turns (i.e., which nobody bothers about), then the soul, too, should not be judged because without the body, no sin could be committed by it. This is what Antoninus said to Rabbi: "The body and the soul can both free themselves from Judgment."[51]

10. One might raise here the subtle objection (*ve-ʾim yesh medaqdeqin ve-ʾomrin*) that as, in fact, the body is but a tool in respect to the soul, and if the body is judged in accordance with the action it has committed—[we must conclude] that the sword itself, or the bow or any other tool used by [man] to perform an action, ought also to be judged. The answer to this objection is twofold. Firstly, the action of the human body does not resemble that of his sword or bow or any other tools for two reasons. One reason is that, although the body does not perform any action except through the thought and direction of the soul, the action performed by the body is not due entirely to the mind. For if it were otherwise, it would necessarily follow that the strength of the body would not diminish or increase, except through the strength of the mind. But a tool, which performs its task only through the force of the man who is using it, does in fact perform the work in accordance with the force exerted by man—be it small or great, as well as in accordance with the man's intention—be

it good or bad. You can see [clearly] with your own eyes that the strength of the body does not depend on the strength of the mind; for often when the body is injured, the strength of the mind is not affected. We also know that the human body cannot be forced (against its own will) to perform a deed, as a tool can be forced. Reason, therefore, compels us to conclude that the human body will be judged, but not the tool [used by man]. The second reason is that justice demands that the human body should be judged, and that a tool should neither be judged nor receive a reward. [This is so] because the human body holds life (ruaḥ ḥayyim) and perceives what it is doing, and is aware of doing good and evil, but a tool has none of these perceptions. The second reply is that the human body is not judged on its own, but with its soul, just as it happened when the action was performed. This is also required by the demands of justice, as Rabbi answered Antoninus. Therefore reason forces us to admit that the body will be judged, because it has the perception of being punished or rewarded; the judgment of the body will thus not be in vain. Whereas, were a tool to be put back again in the same position it had when it carried out an action, it would be a vain thing,[52] and God does nothing in vain.[53] It is false to say that He will endow the tool with the ability to feel its punishment or reward. For the rule of justice would be broken; namely, because the [tool] had performed the action unconsciously, but now it would be punished when it is endowed with consciousness.

11. Some of our distinguished contemporaries maintain (admit—modim) that the resurrection of the dead *will take place* in the Messianic era. According to them, the life-span of those who will be resurrected[54] in the Messianic era will be *very long* in accordance with the span of "long life" which will be the [distinctive mark] of the Messianic era, but afterwards they *will die*. The life of the Hereafter will, however, come *after* the Messianic era, when the righteous will then be rewarded, death will cease (ʾein bo mavet), and the wicked will then be punished. [In that life of the Hereafter] neither a body nor a bodily shape exists. Only the souls of the righteous, without a body, [exist in the Hereafter,] just like the ministering angels.[55] They [the distinguished contemporaries] adduce proof for their opinions from

the saying of the sages:[56] "In the Hereafter there is no eating or drinking," meaning that since there is no eating or drinking, neither a body nor a bodily shape exists. *This is* the opinion of Maimonides, of blessed memory, in *Hil[khot] Teshuvah,* Chapter Eight.

12. At first we assumed that his [Maimonides'] reason was that since the body cannot exist forever without eating and drinking [therefore it is impossible for it to exist in the Hereafter]. This [is why] we objected to his opinions in our letter that was sent to Lunel. This is the wording of what we said there, concerning this matter:[57] "If some [people] should [object], saying: how is it possible that a body could exist[58] without eating and drinking, [then I state that] the counsel of the wicked is far from me[59]—[meaning, that such an idea cannot be accepted]. He who has created[60] a body out of nothingness has the power to make it exist without eating and drinking. Was it not that the faithful messenger [Moses] has existed on Mount Sinai [for] forty days and forty nights, without eating bread or drinking water?[61] Elijah too [has existed without food] till he came to Horeb, the mountain of God.[62] The same consideration [applies to Elijah] since the day he was taken [up] until today.[63]

13. If someone should object saying: they will live [the dead will be resurrected], yet [they will] die after being resurrected[64]—'Oh! My soul, come thou not into their secret'[65] [meaning that he does not like that kind of resurrection]. If it is going to happen that the sorrows of Hell would again trap me with their snares into the grave,[66] 'what good will my [resurrected] life do to me?'[67] I would better stay there [and not be resurrected at all. I believe that another death after a bodily resurrection will not happen because] 'the Lord of the hosts hath proposed, and who shall disannul it? And his hand is stretched out, and who shall turn it back?'[68] 'Hath he said, and shall he not do it? Or hath he spoken, and shall he not make it good?'[69] As it is said: 'He will swallow up death forever,'[70] and it is said: 'They that turn many to righteousness [will exist] as [do] the stars for ever and ever.'[71] And if someone should say that the wrongdoing rests in it (*'aven yalin be-qirbah*),[72] let us refrain from believing anyone who says it (*halilah mi-lehaztdik kol medaber bah*). He who creates bodies out of

nothingness before their existence can let both souls and bodies continue to exist[73] after resurrection." This is the wording of my reply on this matter in my first letter to Lunel. In addition to this, there are many similar objections in my last (second) letter [to Lunel].[74]

14. On the same lines (ve-khahenah ve-khahenah), Rav Samuel Gaon, the appointed head of [the] Academy (yeshivah) in Babylon in our generation, obje[cted] to his [Maimonides'] opinions. [Rav Samuel] Gaon[75] was also asked about this [matter] from Ispahan and the land of Yemen, because all of them conjectured, as far as they had understood Maimonides' ideas, that he did not admit at all the resurrection of the dead. [It happened] that some villains, disciples who rejected the resurrection of the dead, had gathere[d] there [in Yemen?]. When the inhabitants disapproved of their [opinions], they [the villains] cited Maimonides in *Hilkhot Teshuvah* to prove their point against the inhabitants. [Therefore], the inhabitants had to ask the Rabbi [Maimonides] about it in order to understand his views on that [subject].[76] And he [Maimonides] answered them, and his answer was very lengthy. He added in it [in his reply] many other points which are not relevant to our subject. Now we state (kotevim) the gist of his reply concerning this subject in a concise form.

15. The first point of that reply is that he [Maimonides] cleared himself, before God and before the Jews,[77] concerning the matter [of his belief] in the resurrection of the dead, about which he was suspected by those who distrusted him. The translator rendered his Arabic text into a very difficult Hebrew: but I will then reproduce [78] here such section of it that seems to me sufficiently clear, but will change, to the best of my ability, the other in order to express clearly the ideas that its author [Maimonides] intended to convey.

16. The following are his statements on this matter in an abbreviated form: "You, the reader, should know that our intention in this treatise[79] is to explain what we ought to believe concerning this important principle,[80] about which a dispute has arisen among the disciples, namely, the principle of the resurrection of the dead, the

belief which is widely accepted (*mefursemet*) amongst our people, and is frequently mentioned in prayers, in stories, and in hymns (*tehillot*)[81] composed by our prophets and prominent sages, and which are referred to in profusion in the Talmud [as well as] the Midrashim.[82] The meaning of it, [the resurrection of the dead] is: the *return of an individual soul into the body after it had left it.* This is a subject about which no dispute has ever been heard of amongst our nation, and which cannot be interpreted (*pitaron*) otherwise than in its literal meaning. It is a sin to think that somebody belonging to our faith would believe in what is contrary to the literal meaning of the term 'resurrection of the dead,' that is: the return of the soul to the body after death. Daniel had already mentioned it in a way that cannot [be] otherwise interpreted (*lefotro pitaron*), by stating: 'And many that sleep in the dust of the earth shall awake, some to ever-lasting life, and some to shame and everlasting contempt.'[83] And the angel said to him: 'But go thy way till the end: for thou shalt rest, and stand in thy lot at the end of the days.'"[84] And he [Maimonides], may God keep him,[85] also said: "It seems to us that those people whose souls will return to their bodies will eat and dring and copu-late and procreate and die after a very long life, similar to the general life span which will exist in the Messianic era."[86]

17. "However, the life after which there is no death is the life of the Hereafter, because there is no body in it, as we believe in that mat-ter; this is considered to be true by every intelligent person, [namely,] that the Hereafter [consists] of souls without bodies, like angels. The explanation of this matter is that the bod[y] is really [only] an assembly of organs (*kelim*) for the actions of the soul. This has already been shown by rational proof. All that is in the body is divided into three parts: organs with which feeding is carried out, [i.e.] the mouth and the stomach. [The latter] is called in Arabic *māʿida*. And the liver and the entrails, and, in general, all that is in the lower abdomen. And organs with which procreation is carried out, those are the organs of copulation and of the production of the sperm and the production of the embryo. And organs by the help of which the body continues to function, so that it can procure for itself all that it needs, that is, the eyes and the other senses, as well as all

the tendons, those which are hollow and those which are not hollow, as, for instance, those tendons which are called in Arabic *'aṣb,* and tendons by the help of which all movements are accomplished, without which a living being could not move toward its food [or] could not escape from that which is hostile to it, and might cause it to perish and damage its constitution. And as [he, man] can get his sustenance (*mamon*)[87] only through actions which he has to perform, and preparations[88] which he has to make, and which require thinking and planning, he was [also] given intellect in order to regulate[89] them, and he was also given natural organs in order to perform those actions, I mean, hands and feet, because the feet are not organs for walking only. The details of this rule are known to the learned men. It has already been made clear that the only reason for the existence of the body is for the sake of absorbing food for the continuation of the body and the procreation of a similar body for the continuation of the species of that body. When that reason [namely, the need for the existence of the body] is removed, because this existence is redundant, I mean [that this is so with respect to] the Hereafter, about which many (*hamon*) among the sages have already explained to us that 'there is no eating nor drinking in it'[90]—this is, therefore, an explanation for the nonexistence of the body, because God, blessed be He, would certainly not create anything in vain, and He would only do something for a specific reason. And God forbid that His well-ordered actions be similar to the actions of the worshippers of images, which have eyes, but do not see; ears, but do not hear, and a nose, but do not smell.[91] So, according to those [people][92] God creates bodies, meaning organs, not at all for the purpose of performing with their help what they were created for, but for no reason at all. Or perhaps they would have us believe that people in the Hereafter, according to the [opinion] of those people, are not endowed with organs, but nevertheless have bodies; and perhaps these bodies are ball-like, or [perhaps they are] cylindrical like pillars, or square in length and width and height, their squareness equal in each direction, like the form of a cube.[93] However, such [opinions] are only ridiculous: 'Oh! that ye would altogether hold your peace. And it should be your wisdom.'[94],[95] And the reason for all this that we have explained is that the masses do not consider any existence [possible] except what is a body or what is in the body. That which is not a body or is not in a body does not exist according to their opinion, so that whenever they want to establish the existence of anything, they associate it with bodies, I mean, they add density to the essence of its body."[96]

The foregoing is an abbreviated version of Maimonides' opinions.

18. And he has also written in that reply:[97] "Other people have also had their doubts concerning what we had said at the end of our *Hibbur* (*Mishneh Torah*),[98] viz: 'Do not think that the King the Messiah will have to perform signs and miracles, bring anything new into being, revive the dead, or do similar things, etc.' We had also brought evidence for the above statement. However, some intellectually weak people considered that [the above passage in *Mishneh Torah*] is a denial of the resurrection of the dead, even though we did not say anything, except that the Messiah will not be asked to perform a miracle—to divide the sea or to revive a dead [man] in a miraculous way—because no miracle would be demanded of him. [This is so], since the prophets whose prophecy is truthful[99] have promised us [the future coming of the Messiah]. From that which has been said [before, in *Mishneh Torah*] it is not to be deduced that God might not resurrect the dead according to His wish, whenever He should wish, and whomever He should wish, be it in the times of the Messiah, or [perhaps] before his [coming], or after his death."

Up to here [we have quoted] him [Maimonides] verbatim. There are also many other points [in addition] to these [quotations] which, by the help of God, we shall bring in this chapter, but which do not appertain to our subject, namely, the Hereafter, which we have begun to discuss.

19. After having quoted his [Maimonides'] opinions on the Hereafter, namely, that the body does not exist in it,[100] we begin by stating our own opinion, and the reasons for it, and to prove that in the Hereafter, in which there is no eating or drinking; nevertheless a body and a bodily shape will exist in it. This is what the scholars among the first Geonim wrote, and such is also the widespread

tradition of all the Jews; [indeed] even the oral tradition, which he [Maimonides] adduced as evidence, serves us as witness that in the Hereafter, about which they [the sages] said that there "is no eating or drinking," body and bodily shape will in fact exist. The reason is, that if there were no body and bodily shape in it, why was he [Rav] compelled to say that all those [functions like eating, etc.] do not exist in it? He should have said that the body does not exist [in the Hereafter], and consequently all those [functions] would have ceased automatically. If he had said that there is no body in it, would anyone have imagined that eating and drinking as well as negotiation and propagation exist in it? We have already explained this matter at the beginning of our discussion.

20. And furthermore, according to his [Maimonides'] opinion, [it seems that] the soul can absolve itself from judgment, [and this brings us back to] the question which Antoninus asked Rabbi.[101] If you say that the bodies receive their punishment and their reward in the Messianic era only, what will their [lot] be in the Hereafter? What advantage would the soul of the righteous have over its body in the Hereafter, since the soul is endowed with an eternal life, whereas the body is not so endowed? Is it because of the quality of the soul itself, which is cleaner and purer than the body? Yet "have not" both "the same father"? "Hath not one God created" them?[102] Is it not that both of them have an equal part in doing righteousness as in doing wickedness? Why, therefore, has the soul greater merit than the body? Furthermore, from a perfect Mishnah we learned about the people of Sodom that "they have no share in the Hereafter, and yet they will appear at the Judgment."[103] It stands to reason that this "appearing at judgment" will take place in the Hereafter, for a text explicitly states: "They will not appear in the congregation of the righteous, but in the congregation of the wicked."[104] It is manifest, therefore, that [the people of Sodom] will have no share in the reward, but will be judged in order to receive punishment.

21. If you say that there is neither a body nor a bodily shape in the Hereafter, you do imply that only the souls of the wicked are judged

in the Hereafter; and [if this is so], how is it that the body of the
wicked gains an advantage over his soul? For in this case the soul
would be judged and get its punishment, but the body would not be
judged and get its punishment! Furthermore, in this case the body
of the wicked would have an advantage over his soul, but the soul of
the righteous would have an advantage over his body! [And the fate
of the body of the just would not be equal to that of his soul!]

22. If you say that the soul of the wicked is cut off when the body is
cut off, [that is to say,] during the era of the Messiah or at the end of
that [era], then who among the wicked would be judged in the
Hereafter? The body would already be dead and the soul already
cut off. And he who ascribes an advantage to the soul over the body
with regard to judgment, seems to imply that reward and punishment in the Hereafter are not according to the deed[s] of people or
according to justice, but according to nature: for the soul, the
nature of which is to endure, will endure, and the bod[y], the nature
of which is to perish, will perish. Hence, the measure of justice
would become defective in both worlds: in this world (ba-ʿolam
ha-zeh) and in the Hereafter (ba-ʿolam ha-ba). [And, moreover, it
would follow,] according to this opinion, that the souls of the righteous and of the wicked are not judged according to their deeds but
according to their knowledge, because the soul which knows its
Creator through rational proof would last forever, because the
knowledge existing is everlasting, while the soul which does not
know its Creator through rational proof will be cut off, although it
may have [the knowledge of the] Torah and good deeds to its credit.
It would follow, then, that Torah and good deeds never give an
advantage, since [the final issue] belongs to the sphere of nature.
[On the other hand,] if you say that they give an advantage, you
must admit that [the issue] is outside the natural events, and that
everybody will be judged according to his deeds, his love and fear of
God, as well as according to his opinions. The body and the soul
will thus be on an equal footing in the Hereafter, since both of them
have had an equal share in performing the deeds, whether these
were good or evil.

23. Moreover, if you would say that Rabbi's [Maimonides'] reason, given in his Letter, is that "since there is no eating, drinking, or intercourse in the Hereafter,"[105] the organs of the body that were created to fulfill such functions will exist to no purpose, and God creates nothing in vain—you will have to conclude, when you consider the matter carefully, that for three reasons the resurrection of the bodies in the Hereafter will not be in vain. Firstly, justice requires that the bodies should be punished or rewarded, just as the souls will, because they both have an equal share in performing a good or evil deed. [Secondly,] you might say, if you want,[106] that the organs will fulfill some kind of functions [in the Hereafter], and their creation [to live eternally] will not have been in vain, or, [thirdly,] they will assure the important task of informing the dwellers of the earth of the divine power that can maintain alive bodies with no food or drink; and to create organs, the nature of which is to crave for food, drink, procreation, and intercourse, and [then] transform it, so that they will crave for no such things, although they will suffer no defect or accident.[107]

24. And we found an example for this [i.e., a transformation of nature] in the [case] of the eating of the manna: "And he humbled thee, and suffered thee to hunger [and fed thee with manna, which thou knewest not, neither did thy fathers know] that he might make thee know that man doth not live by bread alone, but by every word that procedeth out of the mouth of the Lord doth man live."[108] And furthermore, justice demands that each organ should receive its punishment or its reward in the [same] state as it used to be when its evil or righteous deed was performed. And since[109] divine judgment requires to endow the righteous [with the capacity] to live without eating or drinking and without toil or sorrow, and [to] "feast on the brightness of the divine presence,"[110] which is a very high degree, the highest which exists for any created being, therefore body and soul are equal in this, just as (the measure) of [justice] for both bodies and souls is equal when they will be judged. Therefore it is [according to] justice that both of them [the soul and the body] should be entitled to that degree [of exaltation].

25. I am very astounded, apart from all that, by the words of the Rabbi [Maimonides], who based his idea of the absence of the body [in the Hereafter] on the fact that God does not create anything in vain.[111] If he [Maimonides] can say so [that bodies do not exist in the Hereafter], what will his opinion be[112] about the bodies of the wicked? Justice demands that [God] should create for them organs in which there is craving in order that they [the wicked] should be deprived of what they crave for, as it is said: "And from the wicked their light is withholden,"[113] and this is not in vain. I also wonder how he [Maimonides] would have explained [in the light of his above-mentioned opinion] the Barayta, which is taught in the name of the Tanna of the school of (devei) Eliyahu: "The dead[114] whom the Holy One, blessed be He, will resurrect in the era of the Messiah, will not revert to (their) dust,"[115] unless he would take i[t] (the Barayta) outside its literal meaning, and explain that the term "dead" used in it means not those who are actually dead, but those who will return to the Holy Land from the melting-pot of the Diaspora, i.e., those who are here called "dead" are whose whom God will resurrect in the Messianic era. The passage then, in which it is said, "[They] will not revert to their dust," refers to those who will not return to the Disapora and to the poverty in which they used to live before, illustrating thus the verse: "He raiseth up the poor out of the dust."[116]

26. We do not know, however, how he [Maimonides] would have explained this statement [in the Barayta], or how he would have [answered the question that may] be asked: what will be the [lot of] the righteous during those thousand years, after which God will renew his world, etc.?[117] Furthermore, if the Barayta (Tanna devei Eliyahu) refers only to those who will return from the melting-pot of the Diaspora and who will not go back to the Diaspora; [what will happen to those who will go back?]. Why did [the Barayta] use such vague language? Is it [possible that the intention of the Barayta] was to mislead people? You cannot compare this matter with other matters, written or expressed by way of allegory, because you will not find anything expressed in this way except in two circumstances. The first is when language is unable to explain the matter to the people,

except by allegory and images, as, for instance, the description of God's members [i.e., the hand of God, etc.], who is above all that. Concerning this and other similar [instances], the sages said: "The Torah employs human language."[118] The second circumstance is when the subject under consideration must be kept hidden from the people, as [for example], the subject of "the end," ha-qez, which was told to Daniel [only] vaguely. He was urged to leave the subject vague because, when Daniel was told about it, the "end" was still a very long period of time ahead, and had he revealed to the people that such a long period of time had still to elapse, many wicked individuals among the Jewish nation would have left then the community, just as [they would do it] even today.

27. But nothing of all this is to be found in the Barayta. For even if the latter did refer only to those who will rise from the dust of their poverty and their dispersion, i.e., the Diaspora, meaning that they will not return to the same dust, why did [the Barayta] leave its meaning so vague? Was it to mislead the people by promising them something which was not going to happen? [But], although it is impossible to assert that the teaching of this Barayta is only according to the opinion of those who say[119] that the story of the dead, resurrected by Ezekiel, is in fact an allegory, nevertheless, from the point of view of those who maintain[120] that those [resurrected by Ezekiel had really] returned to life[121] but died afterwards, it must be deduced from the dead resurrected by Ezekiel that all dead will resurrect; and deduce also that the resurrected will die after resurrection. Our answer to the query [how Maimonides would have explained the Barayta is] that he followed the opinion of those who held that the [resurrection of the dead by Ezekiel] is, indeed, an allegory.

28. And furthermore, it has to be deduced from the text that the statement of this Barayt[a] is not a tradition (qabbalah), but a logical deduction (sevarah). For if it were a matter accepted by tradition (qabbalah), how can anybody conceive it possible to make an inference from the dead whom Ezekiel resurrected? Should we, because

those people died after their resurrection, reject the traditional [view] (*qabbalah shebeyadeinu*) that the dead will resurrect during the Messianic er[a]? And should we be compelled to say that all dead who will resurrect will have to die in the end? However, since they said [in the Gemara][122] that an inference can be made from the dead whom Ezekiel resurrected, it seems that the opinion of the Tanna is a logical deduction, and this allows the opponent of that Barayta to assert that the dead whom God will resurrect during the Messianic era will revert to their dust. In any case, this refers only to the Messianic era, but with regard to the Hereafter (*ʿolam ha-ba*), everybody agrees that death does not exist there,[123] as it is said: "He will swallow up death forever."[124] [This is] not for the reason that a body will not exist in it [in the Hereafter], because the Mishnah[125] and the oral traditions (*shemuʿot*), about which there is no dispute, confirm that a body does exist in it [in the Hereafter], as we have explained.

29. If you question our statement that the Hereafter, as it is taught in our Mishnah,[126] means the Hereafter [that will take place] at the end [of this world], after the Messianic era, and that it will be the eon in which the righteous will be rewarded and the wicked punished—a statement we have made on the ground that clearly, according to all opinions, there is neither eating nor drinking in the Hereafter—if you question this statement, because how can it be supported by the verse: "They will inherit the land forever"?[127] What kind of inheritance can this be, since there will be no eating or drinking there? And what kind of land will this be? Will envy exist there, or warfare, or lack of anything, since God has promised them that they will inherit the land, in order to eat its products and take its silver and gold? The reply to these questions is that the whole context shows that the Mishnah must refer only to the Messianic era, in which eating and drinking will exist and that [era] is *called* here "the Hereafter." [The same consideration applies] also to the [term] "resurrection of the dead" to which this Mishnah[128] refers, [that is to say], the resurrection of the dead, which will take place during the Messianic era.

30. Another proof of this comes from Rabbi Yoḥanan.[129] "Rabbi Yoḥanan said: How is resurrection of the dead derived from the

Torah—As it is written 'And ye shall give thereof the Lord's heave offering to Aaron the priest.'[130] But would Aaron live forever . . . so that terumah (offering) would be given him? But it teaches that he will be resurrected, and Israel will give presents to him. Thus resurrection of the dead is derived from the Torah." [Therefore,] the resurrection of the dead should be conceived only [in connection] with the Messianic er[a], not with the Hereafter, because if it were not so, what would the nature of those presents be, since there will be no eating or drinking in it [in the Hereafter]? [The same explanation] applies also to all those biblical verses from which our Rabbis adduce proofs in the Gemara about the resurrection of the dead, as for instance: "That your days may be multiplied,"[131] and the verse: "Then Joshua built an altar,"[132] or the verse: "Thy watchmen shall lift up the voice; with the voice together shall they sing."[133] All those [verses] and others similar to them refer to the Messianic era, and so does the verse: "And many of them that sleep in the dust of the earth shall awake, some to everlasting life, and some to shame and everlasting contempt."[134] These instances show that all this was said concerning the dead, who will be resurrected during the Messianic era, since a thing is understood from its rational context (me-'Inyano). And the verse: "Those for everlasting life"[135] proves to you that the righteous whom God will resurrect during the Messianic era will never revert to their dust, as it is proved in the Gemara further on from another verse. As to the verse: ". . . some to shame and everlasting contempt,"[136] it proves that some of the dead who will be resurrected during the Messianic era will live in order to receive their punishment, because the punishment of the wicked does not begin only in the Hereafter, but [already] in the Messianic era: the totally wicked will duly receive their punishment from that time onwards for ever and ever, and about them it is said: ". . . some to shame and everlasting contempt."[137]

31. And we found similar [opinions] expressed by the prophets. Isaiah says: "And they shall go forth and look," etc.[138] This vers[e] refers to the era of the Messiah, since this matter is learned from its context, as it is written earlier: "And they shall bring all your brethen for an offering unto the Lord out of all the nations."[139] And

Malachi also says: "Behold, I will send my messenger, and he shall prepare the way before me," etc.[140] This [verse] refers to the Messianic era, as is proved from the verse: "And the Lord, whom you seek shall suddenly come to his temple,"[141] and this is the King, the Messiah. And it is written: "And I will come near to you to judgment; and I will be a swift witness against the sorcerers, and against the adulterers";[142] thus the punishment of the wicked is expressed. And the verse: "And they that turn many to righteousness" like the stars for ever and ever[143] means that they will exist like stars, which exist for ever and ever, the same thing applies to those who "turn many to righteousness," who will live in the era of the Messiah. Although it has already been said with reference to them: "Some to everlasting life"[144] [it was necessary to repeat] it so that you should not say that this world [ʿolam zeh] has a finite limit of time, as it is said: "He shall serve him forever."[145] Therefore it was necessary to add an explanation, namely, "for ever and ever," that is to say, that that time is indetermined, as it is said: "The Lord shall reign for ever and ever,"[146] meaning that it is indetermined.

32. We must also explain to you that the phrase "for ever and ever"[147] does not refer only to those "who turn many to righteousness," but it refers also to the wise, and this is the meaning of the verse:[148] "And they that be wise shall shine as the brightness of the firmament; and they that turn many to righteousness as the stars," [thus] all will exist for ever and ever. And it is also written:[149] "But go thou thy way till the end be: for thou shalt rest, and stand in thy lot at the end of the days." This is a verse which proves the resurrection of the dead, for God assigned to him [Daniel] three periods. The first is when he was still alive in this world (ba-ʿolam ha-zeh), therefore it was said to him: ". . . go thou . . . till the end,"[150] meaning, go now until the end comes, as it was said to him before: "Go thy way Daniel: for the words are closed up and sealed," etc.[151] The second period came when he was dying, therefore it was said to him "for thou shalt rest."[152] We found the same wording in the verse: "They shall rest in their beds,"[153] since the death of the righteous means rest for him from the toil of this world. And on the same lines he who praised the dead[154] in Moʿed Qaṭan[155] said: "Do not cry for

the loss that went to rest." In some instances in the Talmud you find that when the death of a righteous person is mentioned they say: "His soul rests."[156] Also the "rest" which refers to Daniel means his death, because he was not alive at the time of the second Temple, in which case we could have said that it refers to his return to the land [of promise]. And furthermore, the end of the verse proves [it], as it is written: ". . . and stand in thy lot,"[157] i.e., that this rest comes instead of the "standing" (*amidah*) [which is a term for resurrection]. And the third period which was disclosed to him: ". . . and stand in thy lot"[158] means the resurrection (*amidah*) of the soul and the body together. If you say that it is the resurrection of the soul only, [then] for what purpose would it be resurrected, seeing that from the moment of death the soul had already gone to its rest, to become "bound in the bundle of life"?[159] [And, then,] in what place would its resurrection happen? It seems that the verse speaks only about its return into the body, and thus we explain to you that this resurrection (*tehiyyah*) applies only to the resurrection of the dead, because it is said with respect to it: ". . . stand in thy lot,"[160] meaning the destiny which is assigned for you and the time[161] which is designated for your work. From here it is deduced that the dead who will live in the Messianic era will not all resurrect at the same time: some [will resurrect] very early and some very late, each according to his degree. However, as to the Hereafter, all will be resurrected at the same time, since the Day of Judgment will arrive for all. This will be the time for each of them to tak[e] his punishment or reward, as is due to him. And this is what the verse says: "For behold, the day cometh that shall burn as an oven; and all the proud, yea, and all that do wickedly shall be stubble."[162] And it is written: "But unto you that fear my name shall the sun of righteousness arise," etc.[163] "And ye shall tread down the wicked; for they shall be ashes under the soles of your feet in the day that I shall do this, saith the Lord of hosts."[164]

33. And since we have explained that the literal meaning of the majority of those verses and the Mishnah[165] concerning the resurrection of the dead refer only to the Messianic era, [it is clear that this is] also the [meaning of] the rest of the verses and the oral tradi-

tions which are generally concerned with the resurrection of the
dead and the Hereafter, [and] we should connect them all, too, with
the Messianic era. [However], how do we [know] about the resurrection of the dead in the Hereafter? It seems to us that in most of the
instances in which the sages referred to the Hereafter, they certainly
meant only the Hereafter [that will take place] at the end, after the
Messianic era. And about that which has been questioned before us
[in the Gemara][166] in connection with the verse[167] "Then the moon
shall be confounded . . ." when compared with the verse: "Moreover the light of the moon shall be as the light of the sun . . .";[168] it
is explained there[169] that there is no difficulty about it: here [the
verse alludes to] "this world," that is to say, in the Messianic era:
". . . the light of the moon," etc., and there [the verse alludes to]
"the Hereafter": "Then the moon shall be confounded . . ." And
according to Samuel, who maintained: "This world differs from the
Messianic era only in respect to the servitude of the kingdom,"[170]
[there is still no difficulty]. The latter refers to the camp of the righteous, and the former refers to the camp of the divine presence.
Thus, you realize that it is proper to refer the term "the Hereafter"
only to the world [that comes] after the days of Messiah. And it is
also stated earlier[171] "[Rava said: how do we know about resurrection from the Torah? Because it is written] 'let Reuben live' [which
means] in the Messianic era[172] 'and not die'[173] [means] in the Hereafter."

34. As to the passage in the Mishnah:[174] "Every Jew possesses a share
in the Hereafter," does it not refer to the Hereafter [which will
come] at the end? For it cannot be said that it applies to the Messianic era, since the [Mishnah] teaches in this connection: "And
those who have no share in the Hereafter are those who deny the
resurrection of the dead."[175] And the Gemara on this has: "And why
such severity? A Tanna taught: Since he denied the resurrection of
the dead, therefore he shall not have a share in that resurrection."
And if the Hereafter which is taught in our Mishnah is identical with
the Messianic era, [the Mishnah] should have said that "he who
denies the resurrection of the dead will not have a share in the Messianic era." Justice demands that if he denies the [existence] of the

Messiah, he should not live [in the Messianic era]; this is according to the rule: measure for measure. However, if the Messiah comes in his lifetime, why should he not have a share in the Messianic era, not having at all doubted the [verity] of the Messianic era? The [rule] of measure for measure will have no bearing in this case. Therefore, it is certain that the Hereafter which is taught in our Mishnah[176] is no other than the Hereafter [which comes] at the end, which cannot be reached by man except through the resurrection of the dead. [This must be so] because [this] world will be destroyed during the interval [which will take place] between the Messianic era and the Hereafter, as it is said [in the Gemara]: "Six thousand years shall the world exist, and one [thousand years more] it shall be desolate."[177] Hence, all living beings will die. (Text corrupt.) And even according to the opinion of the Tanna of the school (devei) of Eliyahu who taught: "The dead whom the Holy One, blessed be He, will resurrect in the era of the Messiah will not revert to dust." They too [according to this Barayta] will not reach the life of the Hereafter without being resurrected. Therefore the sages said that "He who denies the resurrection of the dead has no share in the Hereafter,"[178] because the Hereafter is reached only through the resurrection of the dead, and he, having no share in the resurrection of the dead because he denied it, will have no share in the Hereafter.

35. And another proof that the Hereafter which is taught in our Mishnah is not identical with the Messianic era we deduce from the following Mishnah: "Three kings and four commoners have no share in the Hereafter."[179] If [the meaning of our Mishnah] is "the Messianc era," why does the [Mishnah] speak about the gentiles who will have no share in the Hereafter? The language of the Gemara is very exact: it is Balaam who will not reach the Hereafter, but this does not refer to the other gentiles. And furthermore, from what is taught [in the Mishnah]: "The generation of the flood has no share in the Hereafter,"[180] it could be deduced that other gentiles do have a share [in the Hereafter]. How can this be explained if the Mishnah speaks about the Messianic era? Surely it is to be learned from here that the Hereafter which is taught in our Mishnah is no other than the Day of Judgment, which will come after the Messianic era. Proof

for [the above assertion] is adduced from the verse: "They shall inherit the land for ever."[181] This fits well [into our argument] since the "sitting of the righteous" will take place in the Hereafter. It is clear that since there exists a body [in the Hereafter] it means that their "sitting" is not in heaven but on earth. And since this is so, it was necessary to say that they will live on earth for ever. And it was also necessary to say that the earth was given only to them, as it is said: "For the upright shall dwell in the land, and the perfect shall remain in it."[182] And this is in contrast to what is said about the wicked: "But the wicked shall be cut off from the earth, and the transgressors shall be rooted out of it."[183] And it is also said: "Let the wicked be no more."[184]

36. However, it should be said that "the good which is in store for the righteous"[185] in the Hereafter is called metaphorically: "inheriting the land."[186] The teaching: "He who denies the resurrection of the dead" means a complete [denial] of the resurrection of the dead, that is to say, that he does not believe [at all] in the resurrection of the dead as referred to in the verse: "And ye shall give thereof the Lord's heave offering to Aaron the priest."[187] Ravina and Rav Ashei, too, adduced proof from those vers[es] in Daniel.[188] We have explained above that those [verses] refer only to the Messianic era, and he who adduces proof from them does not intend to adduce proof in regard to the resurrection of the dead which is taught in our Mishnah, that is to say, that [those verses refer to the] resurrection of the dead and the Hereafter which are taught in our Mishnah. [The fact is,] however, that the sages referred only to those who assert that there is no hint at all in the Bible of the resurrection of the dead, neither in the Messianic era nor in the Hereafter. Therefore they adduced proof from those verses in order to show that there is at least a hint in the verses of the resurrection of the dead. On the other hand, the Hereafter is mentioned several times in the Bible, as for instance: "For, behold, the day cometh, it burneth as a furnace," etc. [189] The prophet has already explicitly explained to us in his closing passage that the Hereafter, which is the day of Judgment, will come only after the Messianic era, as it is said: "Behold, I will send you Elijah the prophet," etc.[190] And that day is the Day of

Judgment which the prophet has mentioned before, viz.: "For behold, the day cometh, that shall burn as an oven."[191] Hence you have learned that the coming of Elijah will occur in the Messianic era [and] will precede the Hereafter.

37. And thus the subject of the Hereafter is explicitly explained by our teachers by saying, in some instances that "there is no eating or drinking in the Hereafter."[192] It is well known that these instances refer only to the Hereafter, and they do not refer at all to the Messianic era since in that [era] eating and drinking will exist. From there you deduce that in the [Hereafter] resurrection of the dead will take place, as we have already explained several times. As it is said: "Let Reuben live," [which means] in this world, "and not die,"[193] [which means] in the Hereafter.

38. And concerning what is said [or stated] in this chapter (of the Talmud):[194] "Ula opposed one verse: 'He will swallow up death forever'[195] against the other: 'For the child shall die a hundred years old.'"[196] There is no difficulty. The first [verse] refers to the Jews and the other to the gentiles. Let us rather apply here the verse: "And strangers shall stand and feed your flocks and the sons of the alien shall be your plowmen and your vinedressers."[197] You are compelled to admit that these [categories] refer to the Messianic era. For if they would refer to the Hereafter, what kind of cattle would it be, and what would the nature of those plowmen and vinedressers be? Therefore [this verse] must be [understood in connection] with the Messianic era. And Ula agreed with the opinion of Rabbi Yoḥanan, who maintained:[198] "All the prophets prophesied [only about the Messianic era" . . .] namely, on a specific and well-known subject. This implies that, according to Ula, the righteous who will attain the Messianic era will not die, but will pass from peace to peace—from the Messianic era to the life of the Hereafter. However, according to Samuel, who maintained that[199] "this world differs from the Messianic era only in respect to the servitude of the kingdoms," death will exist in the Messianic era, for those[200] who had not died before it.[201] But concerning the verse "He will swallow up death forever" (bilaᶜ ha-mavet la-neẓaḥ),[202] he (Samuel) would explain it in regard to

the Hereafter. And we too, according to our humble opinion, accept
the words of Samuel (nir'in divrei Shmuel be-'eineinu). The Tanna of
the school (devei) of Eliyahu was as precise as [Samuel], because he
taught that "the *dead* whom the Holy One, blessed be He, will
resurrect in the era of the Messiah [will not revert to dust],[203] *not* "the
righteous [will resurrect] in the era of the Messiah."

39. Concerning the following text in the Gemara: "Rabbi Ḥiyya bar
Abba said in Rabbi Yoḥanan's name:[204] All the prophets had
prophesied only about the Messianic era, but as regards the Hereafter 'the eye hath not seen, O Lord, beside thee.'[205] And Rabbi
Ḥ[iyya] bar Abba sai[d] in Rabbi Y[oḥanan's] name: All the prophets
prophesied about the Messianic era, etc., but the sages themselves
[said] 'the eye hath not see, O Lord,' as we have already said.[206]
What is the meaning of 'the eye hath not seen'? Rabbi Joshua ben
Levi said: This is the wine that has been kept maturing in its grapes
since the six days of creation. [This is an analogy of the good of the
Hereafter, which] is kept in store for them, as it is written: 'Oh, how
great is Thy goodness,' etc."[207] This is what the [sages] meant by saying: '. . . kept maturing in its grapes.'" And why is that [good of the
Hereafter] compared to wine, because there is nothing in this world
which gladdens one's heart like wine, about which it is said: "And
wine that maketh glad the heart of man."[208] Therefore it is compared to wine, because that joy [will reach] the highest possible
degree of joy. And what is the significance of "kept maturing in its
grapes"? To tell you that this joy has [never] been tasted by man in
[this] world, like wine which has been kept maturing in its grapes,
untouched by any hand.

40. And there are instances in which the [term] "the Hereafter"
refers to the Messianic era. For example, that which the sages have
said in the end of the [chapter] of the Judges of Robbery (dayyanei
gezelot):[209] 'And thou didst drink the pure blood of the grapes.'[210]
They said: this world does not resemble the Hereafter," etc. This
implies that there is eating and drinking in the Hereafter. These
problems cannot be solved because they are so remote from [any
possible] way of solution. However, they should be interpreted in

connection with the Messianic era, in which eating and drinking exist. It is possible to say that Samuel did not admit it at all. Accordingly, wherever you find any reference [in the talmudic sources] to the Hereafter, in which it is proved that eating and drinking exist there—if it is a matter which can be interpreted, it should be interpreted, but if not—it is clear that it refers only to the Messianic era.

And after having explained the subject of the Hereafter which is taught in our Mishnah, according to its literal meaning, and according to the tradition that was handed down to us by our fathers and our teachers, and according to the widespread tradition accepted by all Jews, as well as according to reason, and according to justice, as it seems in our humble opinion, we resume our explanation of the rest of the Mishnah along the usual lines (*kefi minhag*).

Notes

1. Meir ha-Levi ben Todros Abulafia, *Yad Ramah, Massekhet Sanhedrin* (1st ed., Saloniki, 1798). The Hebrew extract of this work appears as an appendix to this study. I. Ta-Shema asserts that no manuscripts at all from the work of Meir Abulafia have reached us. Even the manuscript that was used for the printing of his Commentary to Tractate *Sanhedrin* has not been preserved. This is rather peculiar in light of the great output of Meir Abulafia as a writer. The work of Meir Abulafia of Toledo, RMA, has been partially preserved through quotations in the works of rabbinic scholars. (*Kirjath Sepher*, vol. 43 (1968), p. 569.

2. I have entitled these pages of the Commentary to *Pereq Ḥeleq* as the *Dissertation on Resurrection and Hereafter.*

3. Literally: "All Israel have a part." We translate "every Jew" because of the modern connotation of the noun "Israel." We prefer to translate *ʿolam ha-ba* as "Hereafter" because this term conveys more of the shades of meaning contained in the words *ʿolam ha-ba.*

4. Literally: The chapter about the share [of every Jew in the Hereafter].

5. "Those who should be burned"—the title of the preceding chap. (9) in *Sanhedrin.*

6. "Those who should be strangled."

7. The printer of *Yad Ramah* adapted the order of the chapters of Tractate *Sanhedrin* which is accepted by the Palestinian Talmud. Maimonides in his *Commentary to the Mishnah* follows the same order. It is obvious that in the first printed edition of *Yad Ramah*, the printer or the editor of the text found some difficulty in arranging the order of the chapters. At the end of *Pereq Ḥeleq* he states that this is the end of chapter *ha-neḥnaqin* and not of *Pereq Ḥeleq*, but chapter *ha-neḥnaqin* is missing

altogether. The order of the chapters of Tractate *Sanhedrin* in the printed editions of the Palestinian Talmud is: *ʾElu hen ha-nisrafin, Pereq Ḥeleq* (the tenth chapter), *ʾelu hen ha-nehnaqin*. The order in the printed editions of the Babylonian Talmud is different: *ʾElu hen ha-nisrafin, ʾelu hen ha-nehnaqin, Pereq Ḥeleq* (the eleventh chapter). See also H. Albeck, *Mishnah*, p. 168.

8. *B. Sanhedrin* 99a, *Avot* 3:15.

9. Jer. 32:19.

10. Literally: In the hands of every member of Israel.

11. "Mishnayot."

12. Derived from *sh maʿ*, to hear.

13. *Avot* 4:21.

14. *B. Sanhedrin* 64b, 90b; *Pesaḥim* 93b; *Kritot* 7b.

15. Num. 15:31.

16. The King James Version of the Bible reads: "That soul shall utterly be cut off."

17. *B. Sanhedrin* 90a.

18. Read *ve-khen* instead of *ve-khi*.

19. *Avot* 4:21.

20. *B. Sanhedrin* 107b.

21. Ibid.

22. "Mishnayot."

23. Literally: Sayings of the Talmud.

24. Literally: All Israel.

25. Can also be understood as "rise."

26. *B. Sanhedrin* 91a.

27. We continue to quote the whole anecdote.

28. Ps. 50:4.

29. *Avot* 4:22.

30. *B. Sanhedrin* 90a.

31. Literally: Measure for measure.

32. *B. Sanhedrin* 91b.

33. Num. 15:31.

34. The King James Version reads: "That soul shall utterly be cut off."

35. Ps. 84:5.

36. *B. Sanhedrin* 91b.

37. Ps. 84:5.

38. Literally: The Hereafter includes resurrection.

39. *B. Berakhot* 17a.

40. The text reads: will become, *ve-ʾim hen ha-geviyyot ḥayyot*.

41. *B. Berakhot* 17a.

42. Dan. 12:2.

43. Ps. 50:2.

44. *B. Sanhedrin* 91a. See above, 5.

45. "Mishnayot."

46. *Shemuʿot* may also mean "deduction" or "teaching."

47. Literally: In the hand of every member of Israel.

48. Saadiah Gaon, *Sefer ha-ʾEmunot ve-ha-Deʿot,* chap. 7.

49. This is probably a hint at Rav Hai Gaon's response, and certainly a reference to *Kitāb-al-rasāʾil.*

50. M. Abulafia, *Kitāb,* p. 14.

51. *B. Sanhedrin* 91a. See above, 5.

52. The text reads: would *not* be a vain thing.

53. *Treatise* 10.

54. Literally: will live.

55. *M.T. Book of Knowledge, Hilkhot Teshuvah* 8.

56. *B. Berakhot* 17a.

57. M. Abulafia, *Kitāb,* p. 14.

58. Literally: stand, *yaʿamid,* in the original (r. *yaʿamod*).

59. Job 22:18.

60. Literally: brings into being, *mamẓiʾ.*

61. Exod. 34:28.

62. 1 Kings 19:8.

63. 2 Kings 1:11.

64. Literally: stand, rise.

65. Gen. 49:6.

66. Based on 2 Sam. 22:6.

67. Gen. 27:46.

68. Isa. 14:27.

69. Num. 23:19.

70. Isa. 25:8.

71. Dan. 12:3.

72. The components of this sentence are not parts of biblical verses.

73. *Lehaʿamid.*

74. M. Abulafia, *Kitāb,* pp. 50 ff.

75. The text reads: *Sheʾalunu,* which means: "we were asked." This is a mistake; the text should read *sheʾaluhu,* which means: "he was asked."

76. *Treatise* 15, 16, 17.

77. Num. 32:22: ". . . and be guiltless before the Lord and before Israel."

78. Literally: I write.

79. *Treatise on the Resurrection.*

80. Literally: corner (*pinnah*).

81. The original text seems to have *teḥillot* instead of *tehillot.*

82. The text reads: ". . . the Talmud . . . and . . . are full of it, *maleʾu . . . ʿinyanah.*"

83. Dan. 12:2.

84. Ibid. 13.

85. The text reads *n'r;* it is Aramaic: *naṭreyhu raḥmana.*

86. *Treatise* 23.

87. Misprint in the text for *mazon*, i.e., food.

88. *Hazmanot* in the text is a misprint for *hakhanot*.

89. The Hebrew *lizkhor* (to memorize) in the text is due to a misreading of the Arabic term. S. *Treatise* 24.

90. *B. Berakhot* 17a.

91. Ps. 115:5-6.

92. I.e., those who believe in the resurrection of bodies.

93. Read *qubiyyah* instead of *he-ʿaqev*.

94. Job 13:5.

95. *Treatise* 25.

96. *Treatise* 26.

97. *Treatise* 30.

98. *M.T. Book of Judges, Hilkhot Melakhim* 11:3.

99. I read *neʾemanah* instead of *neʾemrah*.

100. The text reads: *ve-ʿa harei sadero devarav be-ʿinyan ha-ʿolam ha-ba,* which may be the printer's remark.

101. *B. Sanhedrin* 91a.

102. Mal. 2:10.

103. *B. Sanhedrin* 107b.

104. Ibid.

105. *Treatise* 9, 10.

106. Read: *Ve ʾim tirzeh lomar.*

107. Read: *meʾoraʿ* instead of *ʾoraʿ.*

108. Deut. 8:3.

109. *Ve-ḥeivan* is a printer's mistake for *ve-kheivan.*

110. *B. Berakhot* 17a.

111. *Treatise* 9, 25.

112. Literally: what will he do.

113. Job 38:15.

114. Our text changes the word *zadiqim* (righteous) to *metim* (dead).

115. *B. Sanhedrin* 92a; *Seder Eliyahu Rabba,* ed. Friedmann, pp. 46 and 164.

116. 1 Sam. 2:8.

117. *B. Sanhedrin* 92b, 97b.

118. *B. Berakhot* 31b, *B. Sanhedrin* 64b, 90b; *B. Kiddushin* 17b.

119. *B. Sanhedrin* 92b.

120. Ibid.

121. *Hayu* is a printer's mistake for *ḥayu.*

122. *B. Sanhedrin* 92b.

123. *Sha* is a printer's mistake for *sham.*

124. Isa. 25:8.

125. "Mishnayot."

126. *B. Sanhedrin* 90a.

127. Isa. 60:21.

128. *B. Sanhedrin* 90a.

129. Ibid, 90b.
130. Num. 18:28.
131. Deut. 11:21.
132. Josh. 8:30.
133. Isa. 52:8.
134. Dan. 12:3.
135. Ibid.
136. Ibid.
137. Ibid.
138. Isa. 66:24.
139. Isa. 66:20.
140. Mal. 3:1.
141. Ibid.
142. Mal. 3:5.
143. Dan. 12:3.
144. Ibid.
145. Exod. 21:6.
146. Exod. 15:18.
147. Dan. 12:3.
148. Ibid.
149. Dan. 12:13.
150. Ibid.
151. Dan. 12:9.
152. Dan. 12:13.
153. Isa. 57:2.
154. *B. Mo‘ed Qaṭan* 25b reads: *bekhu la’aveilim velo’ la’aveidah.* Our text reads *s. p. q.,* which is a printer's mistake for *s p d* (*ha-sophed*).
155. Ibid. 25b.
156. *B. Mo‘ed Qaṭan* 25a.
157. Dan. 12:13.
158. Ibid.
159. 1 Sam. 25:29.
160. Dan. 12:13.
161. Misspelled with *ṭeit* instead of *tav.*
162. Mal. 4:1.
163. Ibid.
164. Mal. 4:3.
165. "Mishnayot."
166. *B. Sanhedrin* 91b.
167. Isa. 24:23.
168. Isa. 30:26.
169. *B. Sanhedrin* 91b.
170. Ibid.
171. *B. Sanhedrin* 92a.

172. The Talmud has *ha-ʾolam ha-zeh,* "this world," and not "the Messianic era."

173. *Deut.* 33:6.

174. *B. Sanhedrin* 90a.

175. Ibid.

176. Ibid.

177. *B. Sanhedrin* 97a.

178. *B. Sanhedrin* 90a.

179. Ibid.

180. *B. Sanhedrin* 107b.

181. Isa. 60:21.

182. Prov. 2:21.

183. Ibid. 22.

184. Ps. 104:35.

185. *M.T. The Book of Knowledge, Hilkhot Teshuvah* 8.

186. Isa. 60:21.

187. Num. 18:28, *B. Sanhedrin* 90b.

188. *B. Sanhedrin* 92a.

189. Mal. 3:19.

190. Mal. 4:5.

191. Mal. 4:1.

192. *B. Berakhot* 17a.

193. Deut. 33:6.

194. *B. Sanhedrin* 91b.

195. Isa. 25:8.

196. Isa. 65:20.

197. Isa. 61:5.

198. *B. Sanhedrin* 99a.

199. *B. Sanhedrin* 91b, 99a.

200. The text reads *lefi* instead of *lemi.*

201. Literally: another time.

202. Isa. 25:8.

203. *B. Sanhedrin* 92a.

204. *B. Sanhedrin* 99a.

205. Isa. 64:3.

206. This is another version of the preceding passage and interrupts the flow of the discussion.

207. Ps. 31:19.

208. Ps. 104:15.

209. *B. Ketubot* 111b.

210. Deut. 32:14.

4

Analysis of the Dissertation on
Resurrection and Hereafter
in Yad Ramah

The English translation in the preceding chapter is that of the
Hebrew original, preserved in a single source, the printed edition of
Yad Ramah (Saloniki, 1798), where it occupies folios 91b–94b (the
number 96a on the last page is a printing error); it is reproduced
here in the Appendix. Since this text is not at all in the form and
style of a Commentary on the Babylonian Tractate *Sanhedrin*, like the
rest of *Yad Ramah*, and is devoted entirely to the topic of "Resurrection and Hereafter," it must be regarded as an independent literary
composition and as an intrusion from outside into the body of *Yad
Ramah*. For the sake of clarity, I have entitled this independent text
A Dissertation on Resurrection and Hereafter, and have also numbered,
both in the reproduction of the original text and in the Hebrew version, the paragraphs in to which the original text is broken up, as
well as the smaller units that in my view ought to be distinguished
within some paragraphs. I shall therefore refer to the single paragraphs of this work as *Dis.*, followed by the appropriate numbers.

The place in *Yad Ramah*, a Commentary on Babylonian Talmud
Sanhedrin, where the *Dissertation* has been inserted, raises a few problems. After the conclusion of the Commentary on chapter 9 of *Sanhedrin* (fol. 97b, col. 2), follows—as usual in the Babylonian Talmud—the title of the next chapter, 10 (*'Elu ha-neḥnaqin*); but instead
of the expected Commentary on the talmudic text, we find a "Notice
from the editor to the 'dear' reader." Then comes, quite un-
expectedly, the title *Pereq Ḥeleq*, which is that of chapter 10 in the
Palestinian Talmud and of chapter 11 in the Babylonian Talmud; or
in other words, after chapter 10 the sequence of chapters, although
not the text itself, becomes in *Yad Ramah* Palestinian, and no longer

Babylonian.[1] The text that follows upon the title *Pereq Ḥeleq* begins, indeed, by quoting the first sentence of the Mishnah *Sanhedrin* 10 [or 11] in the following version: "Every Jew possesses a share in the Hereafter," etc.[2] and then embarks on a display of reasons and arguments to plead that the proper place of *Pereq Ḥeleq* is *before,* not *after,* the chapter *'Elu ha-neḥnaqin.* There is, however, not the slightest trace of a proper commentary on the text of the Mishnah, and I suggest that the quotation from Sanhedrin 10:1, followed by the conclusion that *Pereq Ḥeleq* ought to follow upon chapter 11, which forms the first paragraph of the *Dissertation,* serves a double purpose: to justify its inclusion in *Yad Ramah* at a point where it could not escape the eyes of the students, and to forge a link with the contents of the *Dissertation* by quoting the first sentence of the Mishnah with the key-word: "Hereafter."

The editor of *Yad Ramah* must have found in the MS, used for the point, the strange typographical layout, with two different chapter titles following each other and the anomalous sequence of a text of the Babylonian *Sanhedrin* having *Pereq Ḥeleq* after chapter 11; for he tells the readers at once that they will find the chapter *'Elu ha-neḥnaqin* at the end of the volume, not where they would expect it, and he explains that he left things as they are in order to abide with the wishes of the author, R. Meir.[3] Now—since in the whole text of *Yad Ramah* no mention of the name of its author occurs, and since it is safe to assume that an eighteenth-century editor of a text could not have had direct information from an author who lived a few centuries earlier, and that no other source of information was available to the editor, who tells us in his "Notice" that he searched in vain to find another copy of *Yad Ramah*—it must be concluded that the editor, Jehiel Jacob Eliakim of Jerusalem (quite a scholar, as appears from his composition, printed on the title page of *Yad Ramah*), had deduced the name of the author as Meir from the circumstance that verbatim quotations from "Letters to Lunel" sent by Meir ha-Levi Abulafia, are included in *Dis.* 12–14, and although this name is not mentioned at all, the author of the *Dissertation* introduces the quotation with a reference in the first person— as, for example, "in our Letter sent to Lunel," etc. The contents of the *Dissertation,* as will be soon seen, are perhaps later than the first half of the thirteenth century, the period of Meir Abulafia's activity. The editor of *Yad Ramah* allowed himself to be misled, although, perhaps, not without some diffidence. For on the title page of *Yad Ramah*, he did not put first the name of the author (which he should certainly have done, had he found such explicit information in the MS which he edited), followed by the title of the book. He put the title of the book first (in square characters), *Yad Ramah*, and underneath it, as part of the title, *Massekhet Sanhedrin*. But then he continued, as part of his own preface, and no longer as part of the title: "*Liqdosh Adonai . . . rabeinu* Meir ha-Levi, *ha-mekhuneh* Abulafia, etc., of the holy in God . . . our Master Meir ha-Levi, surnamed Abulafia, etc."[4] The editor seems to have clearly distinguished, though in an indirect manner, between his own deductions (in which he believed) and what he found in the MS.

Only a very tenuous link connects the first with the second paragraph of the *Dissertation;* the latter paragraph repeats verbatim the first sentence of Mishnah *Sanhedrin* 10:1, already quoted in the previous paragraph, and then plunges straight into an exposition of the doctrine of the Hereafter, not on a commentary of the mishnaic or talmudic text: "The subject of the Hereafter is a fundamental article [of faith] in the Torah. [This premise must be accepted] since he who denies it, even if he may have the knowledge of the Torah and good deeds to his credit, he will have no share in the Hereafter, as is explicitly stated in the Mishnah and further clarified in the Gemara" (*Dis.* 2). This statement is the author's private explanation of the subject of the Hereafter and does not exist in talmudic sources. It is strange that he should assert that it "is explicitly stated in the Mishnah and further clarified in the Gemara." The Mishnah of *Pereq Heleq* mentions only those who deny resurrection, or revelation of the Torah, and the epicurean. The statements in the Gemara on *Pereq Heleq* which deal with *tehiyyat ha-metim* (resurrection of the dead) are based on Midrash and not on Halakha. The style of the statement "since he who denies," etc. imitates that of a Mishnah in Tractate *Sanhedrin:* "he who defiles sacred food, despises the festivals, negates the covenant of our father Abraham, gives an interpretation of the Torah not according to the Halakha, or publicly shames his neighbor, even if he may have the knowledge of the

Torah, and good deeds to his credit, he will have no share in the Hereafter."[5] It is obvious that the author of the *Dissertation* deliberately changed the text of the Mishnah, which says that he who does not believe in resurrection has no share in the Hereafter, and does not maintain that "he who does not believe in the Hereafter has no share in it." Moreover, there is no reference in the Mishnah to any articles of belief. The author of the *Dissertation* mentions neither the text of Maimonides' Commentary of *Pereq Ḥeleq* nor the Introduction to that Commentary. It is intriguing speculation that if the author were acquainted with the Introduction, which includes a passage on resurrection, a major part of the *Dissertation* would have been redundant. I am unable to suggest an answer to this question. The *Dissertation* connects the subject of the Hereafter with a certain, as yet unnamed, controversy: "[We shall] not strive to perform extraordinary deeds or search for great things, nor shall we question the tradition of our fathers, nor make any innovations with our limited and mean intelligence nor investigate the secrets that belong to the Lord our God. The 'what' and 'why' of such matters are not of our concern" (*Dis.* 2). Despite this declaration, the author goes on to discuss the subject, at least, at enthusiastic length!

In the paragraph that follows (*Dis.* 3), the author establishes two points: the first is that the Hereafter is the "period of time that will follow several years after the Messianic era." The second is that "the substantial reward for the righteous and the punishment of the wicked will take place only *then*" (*Dis.* 3), meaning in the Hereafter, and that reward and punishment are *not* meant in *all* instances in which the term "Hereafter" is mentioned. Sometimes the term means punishment only, as in the text of our Mishnah: "The people of Sodom have no share in the Hereafter," i.e., they will be punished by being excluded from it. Contrariwise, in the text of the Mishnah "that every Jew possesses a share in the Hereafter," it means reward only. On the other hand, however, whenever the term "the life of the Hereafter" is mentioned, it always means reward only. According to the author of the *Dissertation,* the Hereafter is a future historical event which will follow after the Messianic era. This is part of the general view on eschatology in the *Dissertation,* a view that stands in evident contrast with Maimonides' opinion that the

Hereafter exists permanently and is a part of the nature of the present world.

Maimonides' distinction between the Messianic era and the Hereafter is utterly different from the theory of the *Dissertation*. The author of the latter develops his theory on the Hereafter by introducing a new meaning into the term "Hereafter" used in our Mishnah, and he often refers to the sources in a general way: ". . . according to the literal meaning of the Mishnah and the Talmud, and . . . to the widespread tradition accepted by all Jews . . . both bodies and souls together . . . will appear at the judgment" (*Dis.* 5). To support his idea that judgment will be done to the body and the soul together, just as they used to be before death, the author refers to his previous statement (*Dis.* 5): "We have already written that reward . . . and punishment . . . will [take place] only in the Hereafter," and adds to it a partial quotation from the anecdote about Antoninus and Rabbi.[6] This haggadic text is the only argument from the Gemara brought up by the author to prove his theory of corporeal existence in the Hereafter.[7] The *Dissertation* alludes to that source several times. The author uses the term *ʿamidat ha-geviyyot ve-ha-nefashot la-din,* the literal meaning of which is the *standing* or *rising* of bodies and souls. He believes that body and soul must be judged together. However, the "standing" or "rising" could also be understood, in that context, as the actual rising of a dead individual from his tomb, namely, his resurrection. The author's intention is to emphasize that the Day of Judgment depends on bodily resurrection, and to make a connection between the terms *ʾolam ha-ba* (the Hereafter) and *yom ha-din* (the Day of Judgment). An additional proof for the latter assertion is found by the author in the saying ". . . the dead will become alive and the living will be judged," and this is followed by a quotation from the Gemara on *Pereq Ḥeleq:* ". . . he who denies resurrection . . . will . . . have no share in the resurrection." "Hence you have learned," says the *Dissertation,* "that the 'Hereafter,' mentioned in our Mishnah, *is* the resurrection of the dead" (*Dis.* 5). Thus, he interprets the Gemara for his own purpose, that is to say, that "resurrection" becomes equivalent to "Hereafter" and "Day of Judgment." Such a conception is the exact opposite of Maimonides' opinions in Chapter Eight, *Hilkhot Teshuvah.*

The source used by Maimonides in Chapter Eight as proof for
his own view is the traditional interpretation in the Gemara[8] of the
verse "that soul shall utterly be cut off" (*hikkaret tikkaret*).[9] The
author of the *Dissertation* uses the same verse, "that soul shall utterly
be cut off," to show that his idea of resurrection is derived from the
Torah, and he joins to it the exegesis of yet another verse: "The text
does not have 'praised thee' but 'they shall praise thee,'[10] thus [we
learn that] the resurrection will take place in the future" (*Dis.* 5). The
author of the *Dissertation* altered the text of the Talmud, which says
merely, "hence you have learned about the resurrection of the dead
from the Torah."[11]

According to the *Dissertation,* resurrection of the bodies is the
precondition of attaining the Hereafter. The talmudic passage from
which Maimonides derived his proof that there is "neither a body
nor a bodily shape" in the Hereafter[12] is also quoted in the *Dissertation* (*Dis.* 6): "A favorite saying of Rav was: In the Hereafter there is
no eating or drinking, no negotiations, no propagation, but the
righteous sit with their crowns on their heads, and feast on the
brightness of the divine presence."[13] But the author of the *Dissertation* does not accept this saying as an allegory, as Maimonides does.
He hints at Maimonides' statement about the absence of the bodies
in the Hereafter to reject it: "If bodies are not resurrected in the
Hereafter, why did they need to say that all those things [eating,
drinking] do not exist in it? They should have said that the body
does not exist in it [in the Hereafter], and consequently all those
[activities] would have automatically ceased. [That they do say so] is
in order to tell you that although bodies exist in it, there is no eating
or drinking. Therefore he (Rav) had to add: "But the righteous sit
with their crowns on their heads and feast on the brightness of the
divine presence." It is then explained in the *Dissertation* that Rav
added this description because "if there are no bodily activities,
from what do the righteous derive their enjoyment and what kind of
reward will be theirs?" [In which case] he answered: "They sit with
their crowns on their heads and feast on the brightness of the divine
presence." This explanation reminds us of RAbaD's objection to
Maimonides' deduction in Chapter Eight. RAbaD does not, however, expound himself the talmudic passage, but rejects Mai-

monides' allegorical interpretation: "I swear that this was not the opinion of the sages, when they said . . . 'In the next world the righteous will arise in their clothes . . .'"[14] The author of the *Dissertation,* too, accepts the literal meaning of the passage.

The next paragraph of the Dissertation deals with "the Day of Judgment"; here the author quotes both from Daniel: "And many of them that sleep in the dust of the earth shall awake, some to everlasting life and some to shame and everlasting contempt,"[15] and [from Psalms]: "He shall call to the heavens from above and to the earth, that he may judge his people."[16] Thus, he combines the idea of the Day of Judgment with that of the resurrection of the dead in order to conclude that: "The Day of Judgment makes no sense unless the resurrection of the dead [takes place]" (*Dis. 7*). This claim is supported by the mention of Rabbi's answer to Antoninus,[17] although the text of the anecdote is not quoted. It must be emphasized again that the anecdote is Midrash, not Halakha. At this point the author sums up his conclusion "that the Hereafter, in which the righteous will be rewarded and the wicked punished, is inconceivable without a body." Thus, the chronological order of events in the eschatological eon will be: The Messianic era, the resurrection of the dead, and the Day of Judgment. The last two stages form part of the Hereafter, which, according to the author, is an actual place, where the righteous in their bodies will enjoy life, although no bodily activities will take place in it.

The author of the *Dissertation* concludes the exposition of his view with the assertion that "such is also the widespread oral tradition of all Jews, a teaching received by Moses on Sinai" (*Dis. 7*), and that "Saadiah Gaon also expressed himself in the same [way] in his *Book of Beliefs,*" as well as, "all the Geonim in their books expressed themselves to the same effect." He obviously refers to chapter 7 of the *Book of Beliefs* which deals with resurrection.[18] There is no doubt that the author of the *Dissertation* had made use of the *Book of Beliefs,* where we read, among other arguments on resurrection, "Reward and punishment in the Hereafter is meted out to the body and soul united, since they constitute together a single agent."[19] Although the author of the *Dissertation* does not quote directly from the *Book of Beliefs,* he echoes that text in his exposition, as, for example, when he quotes from the conversation between Antoninus and Rabbi.[20] It seems that when the author speaks about "all the Geonim," he refers also to Rav Hai Gaon (d. 1038) in addition to Saadiah Gaon (d. 942), whom he had already mentioned. There exists, in fact, a reply from Hai Gaon to the question: "How will redemption and resurrection take place, and what will the new sky be like?"[21] It seems that Hai Gaon accepted some of the ideas which are expressed in the *Book of Beliefs*. The author of the *Dissertation* may, however, when mentioning "Geonim," allude to opinions expressed by various personalities in the compilation *kitāb-al-rasāiᵓl*, a passage of which is quoted in the *Dissertation* itself (*Dis.* 8): "If bodies are not resurrected, what hope can they have? Who can expect any hope for them? Who will compensate for its integrity and its trespasses? The body did it, who will give it the reward?"[22]

The author then proceeds to compare in detail the functions of the body with that of a tool: "One might raise here the subtle objection that as, in fact, the body is like a tool in respect to the soul, and if the body is judged in accordance with the action it has committed—[we must conclude] that the sword itself, or the bow, or any other tool used by [man] to perform an action ought also to be judged" (*Dis.* 10). The long and superficial exposition of this comparison concludes that "reason . . . compels us to conclude that the human body will be judged, but not the tool [used by man]." The author, who holds that a personality is a union of body and mind, explains: "The human body holds life, and perceives what it is doing, and is aware of doing good and evil, but a tool has none of these perceptions. Therefore reason forces us to admit that the body will be judged, because it has the perception of being punished or rewarded; the judgment of the body will thus not be in vain. Whereas, were a tool to be put back again to the same position it had when it carried out an action, it would be a vain thing, and God does *nothing* in vain" (*Dis.* 10). The author thinks that the corporeal existence in the Hereafter is not in vain. He discusses the teleological concept that God does not create anything in vain. That idea is in contrast with the idea which is expressed in the *Treatise on Resurrection*[23] that bodies do not exist in the Hereafter "because God does nothing in vain."[24] At this point we hear an echo of the controversy about the meaning of the Hereafter, at which the author of the *Dissertation* has already hinted (*Dis.* 2).

The gist of the first part of the *Dissertation,* which we have been examining, is that the Hereafter will come *after* the Messianic era. Reward and punishment of *body* and *soul* will take place in the Hereafter. The distinction that the author makes between the Messianic era and the Hereafter is also expressed in the *Treatise on Resurrection,* albeit indirectly, [25] but the other argument about reward and punishment of body and soul together has a parallel at the end of the *Treatise*[26] where it is asserted that reward and punishment of body and soul will take place *after death.*

In paragraph 11 of the *Dissertation* a new point is raised. The author alludes to "some of our distinguished contemporaries [who] maintain that the resurrection of the dead *will take place in* the Messianic era." This passage, which begins with *ve-yesh mi-gedolei ha-dor she-modim,* etc., seems to be a part of the controversy at which a previous paragraph (*Dis.* 2) hints: "[We shall] not strive to perform extraordinary deeds or search for great things, nor shall we question the tradition of our fathers, nor make any innovations with our limited intelligence, nor investigate the secrets that belong to . . . God . . ."

The views which are expressed by the "contemporaries" differ from the views with which we have dealt in paragraphs 3–10 of the *Dissertation.* According to them, the span of "long life" will be the distinctive mark of those who will be resurrected during the Messianic era. Who are the distinguished contemporaries? The author does not identify them. We presume that he alludes to Maimonides. It seems that in paragraph 11 we find an echo of the Introduction to Maimonides' Commentary to *Pereq Ḥeleq.* The motif of "a long span of life" which will be characteristic of the Messianic era appears in both texts. The text of the Introduction reads:[27] "*Vēgam ye'erkhu ḥayyei benei ha-'adam . . . ki be-he'eder ha-de'agot ve-ha-ẓarot ye'erkhu ha-ḥayyim.*" The *Dissertation* has: "the life span of those who will be resurrected in the Messianic era will be *very long* in accordance with the span of 'long life' which will be the [distinctive mark] of the Messianic era . . ." However, whereas the anonymous contemporaries maintain that the resurrection will take place during the Messianic era and the resurrected will die again, the Introduction to the *Commentary of Pereq Ḥeleq* deals with both subjects, the Messianic era and the resurrection, separately. A similar argument to that which is expressed in paragraph 11 of the *Dissertation* appears in the text of the *Treatise on the Resurrection of the Dead*,[28] which text is quoted in the *Dissertation* (16): "It seems to us that those people whose souls will return into their bodies will eat and drink . . . and die *after a very long life,* similar to the general life span which will exist in the Messianic era." Ostensibly, the author continues to quote the contemporaries, but he gradually passes on to quote Maimonides' Chapter Eight. This is how he inserts the contemporaries' assertion on resurrection, and the idea that their theory is Maimonides' theory as well. The following is a comparison between the text of the *Dissertation,* paragraph 11, and Chapter Eight of *Hilkhot Teshuvah.*

The *Dissertation:* "The life of the Hereafter will, however, come *after* the Messianic era, when the righteous will then be rewarded, death will cease, and the wicked will then be punished. [In that life of the Hereafter] neither a body nor a bodily shape exists. Only the souls of the righteous, without a body [exist in the Hereafter], just like the ministering angels. They [the distinguished contemporaries] adduce proof for their opinions from the saying of the sages: 'In the Hereafter there is no eating or drinking,' meaning that since there is no eating or drinking, neither a body nor a bodily shape exists. This is the opinion of Maimonides, of blessed memory, in *Hilkhot Teshuvah,* Chapter Eight."

Hilkhot Teshuvah: "The good which is in store for the righteous is the life of the Hereafter. That good is a life which is free from death, and [is a life] that is free from evil. . . . The righteous are rewarded by achieving that pleasure [the pleasure of the life of the Hereafter], and [they are also rewarded] by [being able] to exist in that good. [On the other hand,] the wicked are punished by [being unable] to achieve that life [of the Hereafter]. [The wicked] will be cut off and will die. . . . In the Hereafter neither a body nor a bodily shape exists. Only the souls of the righteous, [exist in the Hereafter], disembodied like the ministering angels. Since there are no bodies [in the Hereafter], there is no eating or drinking."

The distinguished contemporaries maintain that the resurrected "will die." They also say that the "life of the Hereafter will come after the Messianic era," etc. After this declaration, the author claims that "this is the opinion of Maimonides," etc., and thus he tries to attribute to Maimonides an opinion that was certainly *not* expressed in Chapter Eight. In the *Treatise on Ressurection,*[29] it is stated that resurrection will take place *before* the life of the Hereafter. The author of the *Treatise* does not explain this more fully, apart from stating that this is an article of faith, "as we have explained in *Pereq Ḥeleq.*" Only a part of this statement is correct, because in *Pereq Ḥeleq* the author does not say that "the life of the Hereafter will be after the Resurrection."[30] In the *Treatise,* however, resurrection is not directly connected with the Messianic era, as the case is in the *Dissertation* (11). The *Treatise* discusses the opinion of those who understand Maimonides' description of the Messiah's characteristics[31] to imply the denial of resurrection.[32] The author makes it clear that the definition of the Messiah's functions in *Mishneh Torah* shows that the Messiah himself will not perform resurrection. This is so because miracles are not expected from the Messiah. However, resurrection can take place at any time before the coming of the Messiah, during his era, or after his death, according to God's will. Thus, in a very vague way, the *Treatise* tends toward the possibility of resurrection during the Messianic era. This is, perhaps, an intermediary solution between the assertion of the "distinguished contemporaries," as it is expressed in the *Dissertation,* and Maimonides' opinion, which dissociates the Messianic era from unnatural occurrences.[33]

Let us now recapitulate the foregoing discussion with quotations. *Dissertation* 11 has: "Some of our distinguished contemporaries maintain that the resurrection of the dead *will take place in* the Messianic era. According to *them,* the life span of those who will be resurrected in the Messianic era will be very *long* in accordance with the span of 'long life' which will be the [distinctive mark] of the Messianic era, but afterwards they *will die.* The life of the Hereafter will, however, come after the Messianic era . . . "

Treatise on Resurrection 16 reads: ". . . and we . . . explained . . . that the resurrection of the dead is a principle of the Law and its [meaning is] the return of the soul to the body, which must not be explained. And the life of the Hereafter will be after the resurrection of the dead, as we explained in *Pereq Ḥeleq.*"

Treatise on Resurrection 30: "Other people have also had their doubts concerning what we said at the end of our *Ḥibbur* (*Mishneh Torah*), viz.: 'Do not think that the King the Messiah will have to perform signs and miracles, bring anything new into being, revive the dead, or do similar things, etc. We adduced proof for this as we have [already] explained. However, some intellectually weak people considered that [the above passage in *Mishneh Torah*] is a refutation of the resurrection of the dead, although we merely said that the Messiah will not be asked to perform a miracle—to divide a sea or to revive a dead [man]—because no miracle will be demanded of him. . . . From that which has been said [before, in *Mishneh Torah*] it is not to be deduced that God might not resurrect the dead according to His wish, whenever He should wish, and whomever He should wish, be it in the times of the Messiah or [perhaps] before his [coming], or after his death.''

Treatise on Resurrection 31: ''. . . we have already explained in the *Ḥibbur* our explicit opinion [which has been expressed] by them [in the Gemara], that in the Messianic era nothing will be changed from the course of nature.''

We see that Maimonides' implicit rejection of resurrection in Chapter Eight and his outlook on the Messianic era are handled by the author of the *Dissertation* and the author of the *Treatise* in a similar manner, that is to say, that both intend to show that Maimonides believed in corporeal resurrection. In order to give the impression that Maimonides' opinions on the Hereafter, on resurrection, and on the Messianic era are in a certain way same as that of the *Dissertation* and of the *Treatise,* the author of the *Dissertation* neglected a most important conclusion of Maimonides in Chapter Eight, where he states that the ʿolam ha-ba (the Hereafter) already exists in the present world: ''[The sages] called it ʿolam ha-ba only for the reason that that life comes to a man after the life in the [physical] world, in which we exist through body and soul, and which is bestowed upon every man at first.'' Maimonides' theory does not define a particular place or a specific time for corporeal resurrection. Once a righteous man is dead, his soul continues its life in another sphere of the world, the spiritual ʿolam ha-ba', which is the future of the individual and has nothing in common with the expected future time of the Messiah, which time, in Maimonides' view, has a political significance only. The soul that has reached the highest degree of the ever-lasting life of the Hereafter is, of course, not supposed to return to earthly life, a change which seems to be a purposeless occurrence. Nevertheless, the return of the soul to the body after death is the main feature of the idea of bodily resurrection.

In paragraph 12 of the *Dissertation* we are confronted by a new approach to the problem of the Hereafter when the author begins to argue in the first person: "At first we assumed that his [Mai-monides'] reason was that since the body cannot exist forever with-out eating and drinking [therefore it is impossible for it to exist in the Hereafter]. This is why we objected to his opinion in our letter that was sent to Lunel."

The name "Meir" is not mentioned in the *Dissertation* itself except in the "notice from the editor to the 'dear' reader." Nor is that name mentioned in the Commentary of *Tractate Sanhedrin* of which our *Dissertation* is a part. Presumably, the identity of the author has been established from paragraph 12, where the text men-tions the correspondence to Lunel and also quotes from it. The quoted passage from the letter to Lunel belongs to a whole complex of texts which deal with the polemics on Maimonides' opinion on the Hereafter and on resurrection. We would like to compare the quoted passage in the *Dissertation* with its parallel in the letter to Lunel, with a passage in the *Treatise on Resurrection,* and also with another passage which appears in the letter of the *nasi* Sheshet of Saragossa.

The *Dissertation* (12) reads: "If some [people] should [object] say-ing: how is it possible that a body can exist without eating and drinking, [then I admit that] 'the counsel of the wicked is far from me' [meaning that such an idea cannot be accepted]. He who has created the body out of nothingness has the power to make it exist without eating and drinking. Was it not that the faithful messenger [Moses] existed on Mount Sinai [for] forty days and forty nights, without eating bread or drinking water? Elijah too, [existed without food] till he came to Horeb, the mountain of God. The same con-sideration [applies to Elijah] from the day he was taken [up] until today."

The *Dissertation* (13) reads: "If someone should object saying:

they will live [the dead will be resurrected], yet [they will] die after being resurrected—'Oh! my soul, come thou not into their secret' [meaning that he does not like that kind of resurrection] . . . I would better stay there [and not be resurrected at all. I believe that another death after a bodily resurrection will not happen because] 'the Lord of Hosts hath proposed, and who shall disannul it?' . . . He who creates bodies out of nothingness before their existence, can let both souls and bodies exist after resurrection."

The *Letter to Lunel*:[34] this text differs only in one detail from the quotation in the *Dissertation*. In the sentence "he who creates bodies out of nothingness . . . can let them exist after resurrection," the words "souls" and "bodies" are missing.

The *Treatise on Resurrection* (10) reads: "And there was already someone who contradicted this opinion of ours, saying: 'Lo, Moses and Elijah existed for some time without eating and drinking, while they were still bodies, [and] so will the people of the Hereafter.' 'Is it nothing to you, all ye that pass by? Behold and see':[35] [What a comparison], the bodily organs of Moses and Elijah were not devoid of purpose, since both of them were human beings participating in the affairs of this world. They ate and drank with these organs before the miracle and after it. And how is it possible to compare this with a continuous and endless existence, as it is said: 'In a world that is entirely good; in a world that is an everlasting [world].'[36] How can there be bodily organs in vain [fulfilling no function at all]?"

The letter of the *nasi* Sheshet, p. 419, reads: "And concerning what that ignorant has said, that the bodies to which the soul returns during the resurrection of the dead live forever without eating and without drinking: [this being so] because the creator of man, before [man] existed, will be able to let him exist without eating and drinking. He brings proof for his opinions that the body and the bodily shape will exist forever without eating and drinking, from Moses our teacher, and from Elijah, of blessed memory. [Since] they were alive for forty days and forty nights and did not eat bread, nor did they drink water. [Our objection is that] you should not wonder, if Moses . . . while standing on the mountain of [God], was feasting on the brightness of the divine presence, and could forgo food for a certain number of days. One should not adduce proof from a man who while still alive was similar to a divine angel . . . even if he lived all his life without eating and drinking. How much more so, since he existed without eating and drinking, only for as long as he dwelt on the mountain, before God, and speaking with Him, and feasting on the brightness of His divine presence. But during all the rest of his life he ate and drank like all other people who are endowed with a body and a bodily shape, because this is the nature which God has implanted in man from the day of his creation [namely], to sustain his soul and body (*ruḥo vēgufo*) with food until the soul (*nefesh*) will depart from the body, and then the [body] will return to the dust to be dissolved into the five elements of which it was created. . . . And Elijah [too] . . . 'went on the strength of that meat, forty days and forty nights unto Horeb the mountain of God.'"[37], [38]

The examination of the passage from the letter to Lunel, the letter that was sent from Meir Abulafia to the scholars of Lunel as a protest against Maimonides' opinion on resurrection, and the examination of the parallel passages in the text of the *Dissertation,* show very slight textual differences. The only notable difference, to which we have already pointed, applies to the missing words "souls and bodies" in the text of the letter. This could, of course, be due only to the negligence of the copyist, but it is also possible that the author of the *Dissertation* deliberately added these words in order to emphasize his own angle of argumentation. We should also bear in mind that the words "body and soul" are the key words which change the meaning of the main part of the *Treatise on Resurrection,* when at the end of the *Treatise* we hear that corporeal resurrection will precede the "reward and punishment to the *body* and the *soul.*"[39] From the comparison between paragraph 10 of the *Treatise* and the letter to Lunel, it seems that the *Treatise* answers the objection which is expressed in the letter of Meir Abulafia of Toledo: "And there was already someone who contradicted this opinion of ours (about the absence of bodies in the Hereafter), saying: '. . . Moses and Elijah existed . . . without eating . . . so will the people of the Hereafter."[40] The opinion about the absence of bodies in the Hereafter is the opinion of Maimonides in *Mishneh Torah,* and the author of the *Treatise*[41] quotes it and adds to it his apologetic assertion that "God does nothing in vain," which means that bodily organs would be useless in the Hereafter (p. 94). Paragraphs 9 and 10 of the *Treatise* reflect the interchange of ideas that was the reaction to Meir Abulafia's letter to Lunel.[42]

The example of Moses and Elijah, which appears in all the three sources—the letter to Lunel, the *Treatise,* and the letter of Sheshet— is not new in rabbinical literature of the Middle Ages which deals with the eschatological eon.[43] That example is used by Abulafia in his letter to Lunel to demonstrate his own point of view, that in the Hereafter it is possible to exist bodily without food. Sheshet, the *nasi* of Saragossa, objects to the evidence of Abulafia on a possible existence without food (see above, p. 43): "One should not adduce proof from a man (Moses) who while still alive was similar to a divine angel . . . he existed without eating and drinking only for as long as he was sitting on the mountain . . . but during all the rest of his life he ate . . . like all other people . . . because this is the nature which God has implanted in man from the day of his creation. . . ."[44] The *Treatise* follows Sheshet's argumentation in a shortened form[45] when rejecting Abulafia's objection, in his letter to Lunel, that the body can and should exist without food in the Hereafter. The author of the *Dissertation* expands the theory of Abulafia and says (*Dis.* 23): ". . . the resurrection of the bodies in the Hereafter will not be in vain . . . justice demands that bodies should be punished or rewarded just as souls will, because they have an equal share in performing a good or evil deed . . . the creation (of those organs) will not have been in vain . . . they will assure the important task of informing the inhabitants of the earth of the divine power that can maintain alive bodies . . . transform [their nature] . . ." The author of the *Dissertation,* who speaks in the first person and is thus identified with Meir Abulafia, the writer of the letter to Lunel (*Dis.* 12), justifies his objection to Maimonides' opinion in Chapter Eight by asserting that Maimonides came to his conclusion that there is no body in the Hereafter because there is no food in it. For that reason he had to write to Lunel in order to insist that bodies will exist in the Hereafter in spite of the absence of fool: "This is the opinion of Maimonides . . . (*Dis.* 11). At first we assumed that his [Maimonides'] reason was that since the body cannot exist forever without eating and drinking . . . this is why we objected to his opinions in our letter

. . ." (*Dis.* 12). The connection between the passage in which Maimonides' opinion is quoted (Dis. 11) and the refutation of that opinion as quoted from the letter to Lunel (*Dis.* 12) is very artificial. It seems that the author's intention, in this instance, is to keep up the previous impression about Maimonides' opinion on resurrection—that is to say, that Maimonides does not believe in bodily existence in the Hereafter but does believe in the resurrection which will take place during the Messianic era (*Dis.* 11). However, that kind of resurrection, after which the resurrected will die again, is not enough for the author of the *Dissertation:* "I would better stay there"; he prefers to remain dead than to become alive for a limited period (*Dis.* 13).

A second letter to Lunel, the text of which appears in *Kitāb-al-rasāʾil*[46] is also mentioned in the *Dissertation* (13). The letter contains some arguments similar to those which are set forth in the *Dissertation*. The author of the *Dissertation* alleges that in that "last letter," he, i.e., Meir Abulafia, added many more objections on the subject. A comparison between the two letters shows that the second letter is a repetition of the first letter but contains a longer explanation. According to the author's statement that he had already dealt with the same subject twice in his letters, why was it necessary to discuss the whole matter again in the *Dissertation?* We must agree that the author of the *Dissertation* intended to add some new aspects to the argument which had been brought up in the letters to Lunel. In this connection the author alludes to a link between the contents of the above-mentioned letters and the objections of Rav Samuel Gaon: "On the same lines, Rav Samuel Gaon, [Samuel b. Ali], the appointed head of [the] Academy in Babylon in this our generation, objected to his [Maimonides'] opinions" (*Dis.* 14). The author does not go into the details of the objections of Rav Samuel Gaon. By mentioning the Gaon of Baghdad, the author points out that the disagreement with Maimonides' opinion also arose among Eastern Jewry. This is a new aspect of the polemics which is unknown to the Abulafia-Lunel correspondence. The author's information might have been drawn from the same text that was used by the author of the *Treatise* for his representation of the historical background of the *Treatise*. It is significant that the author of the *Dissertation* does not

admit taking historical details from the text of the *Treatise on Resur-*
rection itself. Some other details that are mentioned as a background
for the composition of the *Treatise* come from Ispahan and the
Yemen: "[Rav Samuel Gaon] was also asked about this [matter] from
Ispahan and the land of Yemen, because all of them conjectured, as
far as they had understood [Maimonides'] ideas, that he did not
admit at all resurrection of the dead" (*Dis.* 14). The text reads "we
were asked" instead of "he [Rav Samuel] was asked" (*she' alunu*
instead of *she'aluhu*). The reading "we were asked" does not make
sense in this context, which shows clearly that the queries were
directed to the Gaon of Baghdad and not to Meir Abulafia. The
above reading could be the result of the author's intention to
emphasize Abulafia's function in the controversy, that is to say, that
even Eastern Jewry turned to him with their questions, or it could
also be a printer's mistake.

The course of events that preceded the composition of the
Treatise, according to the *Dissertation,* is as follows: "[It happened]
that some villains, disciples who rejected the resurrection of the
dead, had gathered there [in the Yemen?]. When the inhabitants disapproved of their [opinions], they [the villains] cited Maimonides in
Hilkhot Teshuvah to prove their point against the inhabitants. [There-
fore,] the inhabitants had to ask the Rabbi [Maimonides] about it in
order to understand his views on that [subject]" (*Dis.* 14). The above
events are recorded in the *Treatise on Resurrection* but in a different
sequence. The *Treatise* reads:[47] "Some of our colleagues from Babylon, sent us letters . . . in which they mentioned that one of the
[Jews] of Yemen asked Samuel ha-Levi, our present head of the
Academy in Baghdad, may God keep him, about those very matters.
He [Samuel] wrote for them a treatise (*ma'amar*) on the resurrection
of the dead." In the *Dissertation* we find a more convincing explanation for the questions which were raised in Ispahan and the Yemen:
". . . because all of them conjectured, as far as they understood
[Maimonides'] ideas." This version is not explicitly expressed in the
Treatise[48] ". . . some people there (in the Yemen), established that the
body perishes and that the soul does not return to the body after
having parted from it, and that the reward and the punishment are
only for the soul. They brought evidence from what we [Mai-

monides] said about the people of the Hereafter (*bnei ha-ʿolam ha-ba*)." The author of the *Dissertation* maintains that "[the villains] cited Maimonides in *Hilkhot Teshuvah* to prove their point against the inhabitants" (*Dis.* 14), while the *Treatise*[49] uses another text of Maimonides which deals with the subject of miracles with regard to the Messiah,[50] at the end of *Mishneh Torah* in *Hilkhot Melakhim:* "Other people have also had their doubts concerning what we said at the end of our *Hibbur* . . . 'do not think that the King the Messiah will have to perform signs and miracles . . . revive the dead . . .'; some intellectually weak people considered that . . . as a refutation of the resurrection of the dead." . . . Another difference between the *Treatise* and the *Dissertation* is a geographical detail. The *Treatise* refers to a disciple from Damascus who doubted Maimonides' opinions, while in the *Dissertation* Damascus is not mentioned. The version here is that Maimonides was asked about the matter from the Yemen (the place of the villains) and that he gave them a long reply. The author of the *Treatise* quotes two different replies, one addressed to the Yemen and the other to Baghdad, the latter being the *Treatise on Resurrection* itself.[51] The author of the *Dissertation* tells about the background of the correspondence between the people who turned to Maimonides with their objections and Maimonides' replies. He also establishes that the prolonged "reply" from Maimonides on the subject of resurrection was addressed to the Jewish community of the Yemen. In that reply "he [Maimonides] added . . . many other points which are not relevant to our subject" (*Dis.* 14). It is possible to conclude, in the light of the above examination of the texts of the *Dissertation* and the *Treatise,* that the author of the *Dissertation* did not know the text of the *Treatise* in its present form. It is probable that he was consulting a text in which there were details similar to those used by the author of the *Treatise* but nevertheless different in certain particulars.

The author of the *Dissertation* states that he will write down Maimonides' reply on the subject of resurrection to the Yemen (as it is understood from the previous description of events), in a concise from; he explains (*Dis.* 15) that Maimonides wrote the *Treatise* in Arabic and that the original text was translated into "a very difficult Hebrew."[52] "I will then reproduce here such section of it that seems to me sufficiently clear, but will change the other in order to express clearly the ideas that its author [Maimonides] intended to convey" (*Dis.* 15). That is to say, the author intended to quote as well as to paraphrase from the Hebrew translation, which seemed to him very difficult to understand. Therefore it is obvious that the author of the *Dissertation* did not know the Arabic text and that he also suppressed the name of the translator of the text into Hebrew. That he did not know Arabic because he admits that he uses a Hebrew translation should be doubted, because he mentions a few Arabic words in his quotation from the *Treatise,* words which do not appear in the Hebrew text of the *Treatise* (*Dis.* 17) and seem to be an explanatory addition to the text. It is more likely that the author of the *Dissertation* was not in the possession of an Arabic text. The accepted text of the *Treatise of Resurrection,* which is ascribed to Maimonides, came down in the form of several Hebrew texts and a few Arabic texts.[53] J. Finkel alleges that the Hebrew text which was edited by him is the Ibn Tibbonic translation of the original Arabic, also edited by him. If this is so, one should expect a text *different* from the text which appears as a quotation from the *Treatise* in the *Dissertation,* because the author of the *Dissertation* claims that he had to paraphrase the style of the difficult Hebrew. However, the text which is quoted in the *Dissertation* is almost *completely identical* with the text that J. Finkel edited.[54]

This means that the Hebrew edition which is edited as the Tibbonic translation cannot be a Tibbonic translation since it is the same text as the one that was "paraphrased" by the author of the *Dissertation.* We hold that the quoted and paraphrased text in the *Dissertation* is the *original* source of the Hebrew text of the *Treatise,* and that the Arabic is probably a translation from the Hebrew.[55] The author of the *Dissertation* asserts that Maimonides began the *Treatise* by clearing his reputation "before God and before the Jews concerning the matter [of his belief] in the resurrection of the dead, about which he was suspected by those who distrusted him" (*Dis.* 15). This is how the author of the *Dissertation* interprets the long introduction and discussion in the *Treatise,*[56] the aim of which is to show that the author of the *Treatise* was misunderstood by the public when he stressed the importance of the Hereafter in his works and discussed it at length, while the subject of resurrection was neglected by him. The author of the *Dissertation* begins his quotation from the *Treatise* with the main point of the exposition of the *Treatise* (*Dis.* 16):

"The following are his statements on this matter in an abbreviated form: 'You, the reader, should know, that our intention in this treatise is to explain what we ought to believe concerning this important principle, about which a dispute has arisen among the disciples, namely, the principle of the resurrection of the dead, the belief which is widely accepted by our people, and is frequently mentioned in prayers, in stories, and in hymns, composed by our prophets and prominent sages, and which are referred to in profusion in the Talmud [as well as] the Midrashim. The meaning of it [the resurrection of the dead] is: the return of an *individual soul into the body after it had left it.* This is a subject about which no dispute has been heard of amongst our nation, and which cannot be interpreted otherwise that in its literal meaning. It is a sin to think that somebody belonging to our faith would believe in what is contrary to the literal meaning of the term, [i.e.] resurrection of the dead, that is: the return of the soul and the body after death. Daniel already mentioned it in a way that cannot [be] otherwise interpreted, by stating: "And many that sleep in the dust of the earth shall awake, some to everlasting life, and some to shame and everlasting contempt."[57] And the angel said to him: "But go thy way till the end: for thou shalt rest, and stand in thy lot at the end of the days."'"[58]

The parallel passage of the *Treatise,* in addition to the above quotation, has the following:[59] "Nothing [new] is added in that treatise to all that we have already said in the *Commentary of the Mishnah* or in the *Ḥibbur* (*Mishneh Torah*), but [the *Treatise*] contains a repetition of subjects, is more drawn-out, and some additional explanation, [so] that even women and fools will be able to understand, but no more." The last passage is missing in the *Dissertation,* but the whole parallel paragraph beginning with "you, the reader," etc., is almost identical with the quotation in the *Dissertation.* The *Treatise* also explains[60] how the above-mentioned verses of Daniel should be interpreted: "And it is my intention to explain to you in this very treatise why we should not explain these verses as we explained many verses of the Torah, differently from their literal meaning."

This passage, too, is not quoted in the *Dissertation*. A close comparison between the quoted text in the *Dissertation* and the text of the *Treatise* shows that every instance in the *Treatise* which relies on the Introduction to the Commentary to *Pereq Ḥeleq* has been omitted. Whereas the apologetic argument in the *Treatise* bases itself on "what we have already said in the *Commentary of the Mishnah* or in the *Ḥibbur*," the quoted passage in the *Dissertation* is independent of any allusions to the works of Maimonides. The author states (*Dis.* 16) that "the following are his [Maimonides'] statements . . . in an abbreviated form." The quotation which follows reads: ". . . our intention in this treatise is to explain what we ought to believe concerning this important principle about which a dispute has arisen, etc. [That subject] is frequently mentioned in the prayers, in stories and hymns, composed by our prophets and the prominent sages, etc. The meaning of it [the resurrection of the dead] is: the return of the individual soul into the body after it had left it."[61] The text of the apology which appears in the *Treatise,* namely, that "nothing [new] is added . . . to all that we have already said . . . but [the *Treatise*] contains a repetition of subjects . . . [so] that even women and fools will be able to understand, but no more,"[62] is omitted in the *Dissertation*. However, the quotation in the *Dissertation* presents a new, totally alien opinion to Maimonides' train of thought as it is expressed in the Introduction to the Commentary of *Pereq Ḥeleq,* in *Mishneh Torah,* and in the *Guide of the Perplexed.* In these works, the definition of the term "resurrection of the dead" as meaning the return of the soul to the body is not to be found. This is the *novelty* of the *Treatise*. The whole passage which starts with "our intention," etc., does not seem to come under the category of a Maimonidean conception.[63] Would Maimonides use a vague reference such as "prayers . . . stories . . . hymns" for proving his theory? Furthermore, a major part of the above-quoted passage, starting with the sentence ". . . which is widely accepted amongst our people . . . about which no dispute has been heard . . .,"[64] appears exactly in the same wording in another text. That text happens to be a continuation of the text of the thirteenth principle (see above, p. 27) which is recorded in a note of Azariah Rossi in his book *Meʾor ʿEinayim*.[65] The text of the *Treatise*[66] explains why certain biblical verses should be accepted literally, such as those in the Book of Daniel, "and many of them that sleep in the dust . . . shall awake," etc., while the text in *Me'or 'Einayim* asserts that the "return of the soul to the body *is a miracle (hu' min ha-nissim)*, and it is very clear and its meaning is clear. We should believe in it according to the true tradition *(ha-haggadah ha-ẓodeqet)*." Azariah min ha-Adummim (d. 1578) tends to accept the passage as an authentic explanation by Maimonides which was added to the text of the Thirteen Principles by Maimonides himself. "His having been accused of brevity in his *Commentary to the Mishnah* . . ." compelled Maimonides to explain his position. "This means," says Azariah, "that Maimonides included here all that he has discussed at length in the *Treatise on Resurrection.*"[67] It seems that except in the *Dissertation*, the longest quotation from the *Treatise* is that which appears in the book *Me'or 'Einayim*. We have before us a text which is quoted in three instances, namely: the *Treatise,* the *Dissertation, Me'or 'Einayim*. Azariah min ha-Adummim maintains that the aforementioned text is the continuation of Maimonides' explanation of the Thirteen Principles. However, this is not the case in the standard editions of Maimonides' Commentary on *Pereq Ḥeleq*. The author of the *Dissertation* quotes the passage, but he does not mention at all Maimonides' Commentary on *Pereq Ḥeleq* or the Thirteen Principles. It seems to us that this passage, which is a key passage expressing the belief in bodily resurrection in the *Treatise*, was written by the same person who tried to prove that this was Maimonides' original opinion. It is rather, a "wandering" text which calls for careful examination. It also seems that if the author of the *Dissertation* knew about the existence of the *thirteenth principle* on *ṭehiyyat ha-metim* he *would have referred to it* as to *Maimonides' concept* of resurrection, but since he does not mention it, we conclude that he did not know of its existence.[68] The author of the *Treatise* wants his reader to believe that according to the passage in Maimonides' Introduction to *Pereq Ḥeleq*, Maimonides explained there that he believes in a corporeal resurrection. As we have shown, this is not correct because Maimonides *does not* explain in that passage the meaning of *ṭehiyyat ha-metim*.

The next quotation from the *Treatise (Dis.* 16) reads: "He [Maimonides], may God keep him (*n"r—natrei hu raḥmana*), also said: 'It seems to us that those people whose souls will return into their bodies will eat . . . and die after a very long life, similar to the general life-span which will exist in the Messianic era.'" The blessing which follows Maimonides' name is in the present tense, and is used when a person is still alive.[69] However, this fact does not necessarily show that the *Dissertation* was written in Maimonides' lifetime. In passage 12 of the *Dissertation,* Maimonides is referred to as of "may his memory be blessed" (*z"l—zikhrono livrakha*), which also supports the supposition that the present tense in the context is not valid. The blessing could have been added by a copyist or by the printer, or it could have been written by the author himself with the intention to give the impression that the discussion took place during Maimonides' lifetime. This point is mentioned here because we presume that the *Dissertation,* as a whole, was written after Maimonides' death, and is a part of the polemics about Maimonides' position on the belief in resurrection. The above quotation "it seems to us," etc.,[70] has already been discussed in this chapter (see above, p. 96). We quoted it again in order to show the passages which the author of the *Dissertation* selected from the text of a certain version of the *Treatise* that he used. The passage in the *Treatise* which admits that in the future, possibly in the Messianic era, a bodily resurrection will take place, is followed by a partial quotation from Chapter Eight of *Hilkhot Teshuvah*. This is how the author of the *Treatise*[71] shows that the previous statement about bodily resurrection is also a part of Maimonides' point of view. This theory also suits the system of the author in the second part of the *Dissertation,* where he establishes the "link" between the opinions of the distinguished contemporaries and the opinion of Maimonides (see above, p. 96–97). The partial quotation from Chapter Eight about the absence of bodies in the Hereafter is followed by the explanation that this fact "is considered to be true by every intelligent person."[72] Next to that self-evident proof comes a long and detailed quotation from the *Treatise*[73] about the functions of the body, which concludes with a statement from the Talmud that "there is no eating or drinking [in the Hereafter]."[74] Maimonides, in Chapter Eight, uses that statement as a proof of the absence of bodies in the Hereafter. The author of the *Treatise* asserts that the very existence of the body is to get food for its own preservation and for the sake of the procreation of the species. There is no point in preserving the human body in the Hereafter, and therefore human bodies will not exist there, because "God would not ever invent (create) anything in vain."[75] The teleological motif, which we have already mentioned (see above, p. 94), belongs to the polemical argument between two opposing parties, the Maimonideans, who assert that no bodily resurrection will take place and that the existence of bodies in the Hereafter is useless,[76] and the Abulafians, who assert that the dead will resurrect bodily and that the bodies as well as the souls will receive their reward and punishment in the Hereafter.[77] The author of the *Dissertation* cuts short his quotation from the *Treatise* at the point at which it explains that the wider public can understand only the actual existence of bodies and cannot grasp an abstraction. The author ignores the fact that the *Treatise* defends its teleological argument with the *Guide of the Perplexed*,[78] and he ends this part of the quotation by saying: "The foregoing is an abbreviated version of Maimonides' opinions" (*Dis.* 17).

Nevertheless, we find that another passage is added in the *Dissertation* to the quotations from the *Treatise*. The idea of this passage is that what Maimonides wrote in *Hilkhot Melakhim*,[79] namely, that the Messiah is not supposed to revive the dead, does not mean that God will not resurrect the dead whenever He wishes (*Dis.* 18). This passage, which begins with the sentence "other people have also had their doubts concerning what we said at the end of our *Hibbur*,"[80] hints at the polemics about Maimonides' opinions without specifying who these polemicists were. It seems, as we have shown (see above p. 97), that this passage is somehow linked with paragraph 11 of the *Dissertation*. Whatever the intentions of the author may have been in choosing these particular passages from the text of the *Treatise*, it is clear that the intention of the *Treatise* itself has been altered. We refer to the above sentence in the *Treatise*, "other people," etc., the continuation of which is in the *Treatise*: "and that it [*Hilkhot Melakhim*] contradicts what we have explained in the *Commentary of the Mishnah* that 'the resurrection of the dead is a fundamental article of faith' [this] is completely explained, there being neither possible doubt concerning it nor contradiction."[81] The author of the *Dissertation* does not know (or ignores) the existence of the Introduction to Maimonides' *Commentary of the Mishnah,* which is alluded to in the text of the *Treatise.*

It should be noticed that in the text of *Hilkhot Melakhim* the term "resurrection of the dead" does not appear, and instead of this term we find the words which denote the very action of resurrection, *mehayyeh metim* ("Thou revivest the dead."). The same terminology appears in the main daily Jewish prayer, the *shemoneh ʿesreh* (eighteen benedictions) (see above, p. 4). We do not know another source, except the *Treatise* itself, where Maimonides was criticized for his opinions regarding resurrection in *Hilkhot Melakhim.*[82] We should bear in mind that the terminology *mehayye ha-metim* is *not* defined in *Hilkhot Melakhim.* The author of the *Treatise* intends to reconcile Maimonides' opinion in *Hilkhot Melakhim,* which asserts that the Messiah is not expected to revive the dead, with the assertion in the *Treatise* that resurrection depends on the will of God. At this point, the quotation from the *Treatise on Resurrection* in the *Dissertation* is interrupted, but the author promises that he will come back to it later in his discussion and bring up more details from the *Treatise* which do not belong to the subject of the Hereafter.

The transition from the second to the third part of the *Dissertation* starts with a further argument on the subject of the Hereafter (*Dis.* 19): "After having quoted his [Maimonides'] opinions on the Hereafter, namely, that the body does not exist in it, by stating our own opinion, and the reasons for it, and to prove that in the Hereafter a body ... will exist." It seems that what we have here is another unit of the polemical literature which has its equivalents in *Kitāb-al-rasāʾil.*[83] In the first part of the *Dissertation* we have already seen that the anonymous author gives several interpretations for the meaning of the Hereafter that is mentioned in the Mishnah, "every Jew possesses a share," etc. Later on the author of the *Dissertation* becomes identified with Meir Abulafia, the author of the letters to Lunel, which letters are a main part of *Kitāb-al-rasāʾil.* Then comes the representation of Maimonides' "reply," i.e., the *Treatise on Resurrection,* and a long quoted passage from the *Treatise* without any direct comments. The third part of the *Dissertation* opens a new or renewed discussion on the Hereafter (*Dis.* 19). The main aim of the author, who speaks in the first person, is to convince his readers that bodies must exist in the Hereafter, although he accepts the talmudic sources as proof that there is no food in the Hereafter. The conclusion he draws from this text is the exact opposite of the conclusion drawn by Maimonides from the same text. He gives a different meaning to the statement of Rav:[84] "He should have said that the body does not exist [in the Hereafter] and consequently all those [functions] would have ceased . . ." (*Dis.* 19). This objection appears already in paragraph 6 of the *Dissertation.* The author bases his proof on the first Geonim, on the widespread tradition of the Jews, as well as the oral tradition, but he does not specify his sources. All these sources are in contradiction with Maimonides' opinion because "according to his opinion [it seems that] the soul can absolve itself from judgment [and this brings us back to] the question that Antoninus had asked Rabbi" (*Dis.* 20).[85] The author introduces a new hypothesis and rejects it: "If you say that the bodies receive their punishment and their reward in the Messianic era only, what will their [lot] be in the Hereafter?" (*Dis.* 20). The author does not reveal the source of the above assertion. The style of his argument suggests that this is part of a wide dispute about Maimonides' opinion on the Hereafter. These are, perhaps, the pro-Maimonideans who introduced the idea of resurrection during the Messianic era, and the author of the *Dissertation,* who in this instance is pro-Abulafian, rejects the idea: "What advantage would the soul of the righteous have over its body in the Hereafter, since the soul is endowed with an eternal life, whereas the body is not so endowed?" (*Dis.* 20). Both the soul and the body are responsible for their righteousness and wickedness, and therefore both should be rewarded or punished. Moreover, if one is to accept Maimonides' opinion about the absence of corporeal existence in the Hereafter, then one comes to the conclusion that only the souls of the wicked are judged in the Hereafter and not their bodies, which is not fair, because this means that "the body of the wicked would have an advantage over his soul, but the soul of the righteous would have an advantage over his body" (*Dis.* 21). The author repeats the previous hypothesis: "If you say that the soul of the wicked is cut off when the body is cut off,

[that is to say,] during the era of the Messiah or the end of that [era],
then who among the wicked will be judged in the Hereafter?" (*Dis.*
22). The author wants his readers to believe that the idea of resurrection in the Messianic era is a Maimonidean idea which he himself
rejects: "He who ascribes an advantage to the soul over the body
with regard to judgment seems to imply that reward and punishment in the Hereafter are not according to the deeds or according to
justice, but according to nature: for the soul, the nature of which is
to endure, will endure, and the body, the nature of which is to
perish, will perish." Therefore, the conclusion is that Torah and
good deeds never give an advantage, "since [final issue] belongs to
the sphere of nature" (*Dis.* 22). The author of the *Dissertation* has
made up his mind about the matter: "The body and the soul will be
on equal footing in the Hereafter since both of them have had an
equal share in performing the deeds, whether these had been good
or evil."

In the next passage the author refers to the *Treatise* to show that
the reason given by Rabbi [Maimonides] for the absence of bodies in
the Hereafter, namely, that "God creates nothing in vain" (*Dis.* 23),
is not valid. The author of the *Dissertation* holds that the very existence of the resurrected bodies in the Hereafter is not in vain. "They
will assure the important task of informing the dwellers of the earth
of the divine power that can maintain alive bodies with no food or
drink . . . and . . . transform" their nature (*Dis.* 23). This is not the
only reason for the actual existence of bodies in the Hereafter. The
author compares the phenomenon of "eating of the manna" to the
expected phenomenon of bodily resurrection, which is also supposed to occur as a change in the course of nature (*Dis.* 24). This is
the only instance in the *Dissertation* where the description of resurrection approaches the abstract. The author goes on with his assertion that "justice demands that each organ should receive its
punishment or its reward in the [same] state as it used to be when its
evil or righteous deed was performed" (*Dis.* 24). He now comes to
the point of his literal interpretation of the talmudic text which is
interpreted allegorically by Maimonides:[86] "And since divine judgment requires to endow the righteous [with the capacity] to live
without eating and drinking and without toil and sorrow, and [to]

'feast on the brightness of the divine presence,'[87] which is a very high
degree, the highest which exists for any created beings, therefore
body and soul are equal in this just as (the measure) of [justice] for
both bodies and souls is equal when they will be judged. Therefore
it is [according to] justice that both of them [the soul and the body]
should be entitled to that degree" (*Dis.* 24). The last passage shows
how the author of the *Dissertation* entwined his theory with the
abstract concept of Maimonides' in *Mishneh Torah:* "And what does
the saying 'feast on the brightness of the divine presence' mean? [It
means] that they [the righteous] know and understand the truth of
God [in a way] which is incomparable to what they can know while
still [existing] in an earthly and base body."

The attack of the author of the *Dissertation* on the teleological
conception is not limited to the text of the *Treatise* itself, but also
raises a hypothetical question which is derived from a talmudic text,
namely, how Maimonides[88] would have interpreted, according to
his opinion, the Barayta[89] which maintains: "The dead whom the
Holy One, blessed be He, will resurrect in the era of the Messiah,
will not revert to their dust." The author of the *Dissertation* says that
Maimonides would have explained it "only outside its literal meaning . . . the term 'dead' used in it means . . . those who will return to
the Holy Land from the . . . Diaspora" (*Dis.* 25). "[They] will not
revert to their dust" refers to those who will not return to the
Diaspora and to the poverty in which they used to live before. The
motif of allegorical interpretation is new in the *Dissertation*. In the
Treatise on Resurrection we find that the author justifies himself for not
explaining certain biblical verses allegorically,[90] but there is no
allusion to the above-mentioned Barayta. That Barayta, as well as
many other passages from the Talmud which are referred to in the
Dissertation, is derived from the Gemara on *Pereq Ḥeleq.* The author
even changed the style of the Barayta[91] by giving the word "dead"
for "righteous" and by adding "the era of the Messiah" to the
original text. These variations in the text of the Barayta fit into the
theory of the Dissertation.[92] The author of the *Dissertation* asserts
that it is impossible to interpret the Barayta allegorically for several
reasons. One reason is that if the aim of the Barayta had been to
describe the return of the Jews from the Diaspora to the land of their

fathers, it would have said so. Another reason is that the Barayta does not belong to that material which is from the very beginning written in metaphorical language in order to be more intelligible. It cannot be compared to the verses in the Book of Daniel "when the subject under consideration must be left hidden from the people, as [for example] the subject of 'the end,' *ha-qez,* which was told to Daniel [only] vaguely. He was compelled to leave the subject vague, because when Daniel was told about it, the 'end' was still a very long period of time ahead, and had he revealed to the people that such a long period of time had still to elapse, many wicked individuals among the Jewish nation would have left the community just as [they would do it] now. But nothing of all this is to be found in the Barayta" (*Dis.* 27). The author of the *Dissertation* claims that the revelation of Daniel was not disclosed to the people of his generation. His explanation for this is interesting: The people of Daniel's time were still too unmature to grasp his eschatological idea, which is expressed in the verses: "And many of them that sleep . . . shall awake,"[93] and "the words are closed up and sealed till the time of the end."[94] This explanation can be compared to that of the author of the *Treatise,* where, in an answer to the question why resurrection was not explicitly revealed in the Law of Moses, he gives a reply similar to that of the author of the *Dissertation.* Due to the fact that the people who lived at the time of the revelation of the Law were as yet unable to grasp the meaning of resurrection, God introduced to them only "the matters of this world, [that is to say,] reward and punishment and . . . about the matter which belongs to nature, i.e., the immortality of the soul or its being cut off."[95] Only after the acceptance of these matters by the people during the course of the generations, when the prophecy of the prophets and the miracles were no more doubted, only then "the prophets revealed to us . . . the matter of the resurrection of the dead, and it was easy to accept."[96] This state of gradual revelation of the miracle of resurrection is compared in the *Treatise* to the gradual preparation of the Israelites, after the exodus from Egypt, for their entrance into the land of promise (see above, p. 38). As far as the *Treatise* is concerned,[97] the idea of gradual revelation in matters of religious belief places the belief in resurrection at the top of the whole Jewish religious structure. If this is really the case, how can it be that Maimonides disregarded the subject of resurrection in *Mishneh Torah?* The same motif of graduality in the conception of religious belief is discussed in the *Guide of the Perplexed,* where it has quite a different connotation.[98] The biblical verse "God led them (the people of Israel) not through the way of the land of the Philistines, although it was near . . . but through the wilderness of the Red Sea"[99] is quoted by Maimonides in the *Guide of the Perplexed* to draw a parallel for the progress of human ideas and morals. J. L. Teicher shows[100] how the author of the *Treatise* transferred the original explanation of Maimonides about the idea of "progress and evolution which is the main subject of his teachings" to the gradual progress in the belief of miracles, i.e., the resurrection of the dead. It might well be that the author of the *Dissertation* uses the same system of explanation which is employed by the author of the *Treatise,* when he refers to the vague meaning of the verses in Daniel: "Had he revealed to the people that such a long period of time had still to elapse (till the 'end'), many wicked individuals among the Jewish nation would have left then the community, just as [they would do it] even today" (*Dis.* 26). It seems that the sentence which reads: "many wicked . . . would have left then the . . . community just as even today" shows the seriousness of the problem. As a matter of fact, the author started the whole discussion in order to justify the literal meaning of the Barayta which asserts that the dead[101] who will be resurrected during the Messianic era will not die again: "It is impossible to assert that the teaching of this Barayta is only according to the opinion of those who say that the story of the dead resurrected by Ezekiel is, in fact, an allegory. Nevertheless, from the point of view of those who maintain that those [resurrected by Ezekiel had really] returned to life, but died afterwards, it must be deduced from the dead resurrected by Ezekiel that all dead will resurrect; and deduce also that the resurrected will die after resurrection. Our answer to the query [how Maimonides would have explained the Barayta is] that he followed the opinion of those who held that the [resurrection of the dead by Ezekiel] is, indeed, an allegory" (*Dis.* 27). It seems that we are able to trace a link between the above-cited text and the text of the *Treatise* which alludes to the same subject; *Dis.* 27 has: "Our answer to the query [how Maimonides would have explained the Barayta is] that he followed the opinion of those who held that [the resurrection of the dead . . .] is, indeed, an allegory." *Treatise* 23 has: ". . . that what was said about him, [Maimonided,] who maintains that the 'resurrection of the dead' in the Bible means allegory, is a famous lie."[102] Nevertheless, the author of the *Treatise* admits that he expressed himself in that way in the matter of the dead of Ezekiel, about which there exists a dispute in the Talmud. We were unable to trace this matter in Maimonides' writings.

The above-discussed Barayta is very important for the author of the *Dissertation*. His intention to prove that the dead will be resurrected during the Messianic era compelled him to add this statement to the text of the Barayta, which does not have "Messianic era."[103] He comes to the conclusion that "since they said [in the Gemara] that an inference can be made from the dead whom Ezekiel resurrected, it seems that the opinion of the Tanna is a logical deduction, and this allows the opponent of the Barayta to assert that the dead whom God will resurrect during the Messianic era will revert to their dust. In any case, this refers only to the Messianic era, but in regard to the Hereafter, everybody agrees that death does not exist there" (*Dis.* 28). It is possible to interpret the Barayta allegorically and literally, "but with regard to the Hereafter everybody agrees . . . not for the reason that a body will not exist in it . . . because the Mishnah and the oral traditions . . . confirm that a body does exist in it [in the Hereafter]" (*Dis.* 28). That is to say, in the future two resurrections will take place, the first during the Messianic era, and those then resurrected will die again, and the second in the Hereafter, in which the resurrected will live forever. The author does not give any specific sources for his final conclusions, but they cannot include the Mishnah of *Pereq Ḥeleq* and the Gemara on it, where the possibility of two resurrections is not mentioned.

The following passage in the *Dissertation* reveals a new aspect in the interpretation of the Mishnah "every Jew possesses a share in the Hereafter": "If you question our statement that the Hereafter as it is taught in our Mishnah means the Hereafter [that will take place] at the end [of this world], after the Messianic era, and that it will be the eon in which the righteous will be rewarded and the wicked punished"—then "what kind of inheritance can this be, since there will be no eating . . . there?" (*Dis.* 29).

The author now establishes a different meaning for the term "Hereafter," as a result of interpreting the biblical verse "they will inherit the land forever,"[104] and says: . . . the Mishnah must refer only to the Messianic era, in which eating and drinking will exist and that [era] is *called* here 'the Hereafter.' [The same consideration applies] also to the [term] 'resurrection of the dead' to which this Mishnah refers, [that is to say,] the resurrection of the dead that will take place during the Messianic era" (*Dis.* 29). This theory is supported by the author's examination of some talmudic passages on the Mishnah "every Jew possesses a share," etc. The author adapts these passages (Rabbi Yoḥanan said: "How is resurrection of the dead derived from the Torah? As it is written, 'And ye shall give . . . the . . . offering to Aaron the priest,' etc.") to his theory, which, among other interpretations, asserts that the eschatological verses in Daniel refer to the Messianic era (*Dis.* 30): "And the verse 'those for everlasting life'[105] proves to you that the righteous whom God will resurrect during the Messianic era will never revert to their dust, as is proved in the Gemara. . . . " The author of the *Dissertation* goes on to explain that "the verse 'some to shame and everlasting contempt'[106] proves to you that some of the dead who will be resurrected during the Messianic era will live in order to receive their punishment, because the punishment of the wicked does not begin only in the Hereafter [but] already in the Messianic era" (*Dis.* 30). The righteous and the wicked will be resurrected in the Messianic era, with the difference that the righteous will not die again, but the punishment of the wicked will start in the Messianic era and will be prolonged from that time onwards. This idea opposes that of the *Treatise,*[107] where the author maintains that certain people will be resurrected but will die again. It also contradicts the view which is expressed in Maimonides' Introduction to the Mishnah of *Pereq Ḥeleq,* where it is asserted that the resurrection is meant for the righteous only. (We have already mentioned that the meaning of the term "resurrection" is not defined in that Introduction; see p. 26.) According to the author of the *Dissertation,* the punishment of the totally wicked will never cease, *le-dorei dorot* (from generation into generation), meaning that they will be bodily punished. This assertion is, of course, the exact opposite of that made by Maimonides in *Mishneh Torah,* where he explains[108] the meaning of *karet,* being cut off, which is the fate of the totally wicked. The idea of an everlasting punishment (*le-ʿolam u-le-ʿolmei ʿolamim*) is mentioned in another chapter of *Mishneh Torah,*[109] where it is based on a quotation from the Talmud. Here again the meaning of the punishment is *karet* (see above, p. 15). The author of the *Dissertation* proves from various biblical verses that resurrection will take place during the Messianic era, but not everyone will be resurrected at the same time, whereas in "the Hereafter all will be resurrected at the same time, since the Day of Judgment will arrive for all" (*Dis.* 32). It is also worth paying attention to the interpretation which is given in *Dis.* 32 to the meaning of the eschatological verses in Daniel: ". . . 'and stand in thy lot' means the resurrection (*ʿamidah*) of the soul and the body together."

ʿAmidah, arising from the tomb, is the Christian concept of resurrection. The same verse is also quoted in the *Treatise*[110] without analyzing its meaning, but the quotation is preceded by the statement of the author that "the resurrection of the dead means the return of the soul after death." This statement may refer to the same meaning which the author of the *Dissertation* gives to the verses of Daniel. The author asserts that the verses of Daniel should not be interpreted allegorically: "Also the 'rest' which refers to Daniel means his death, because he was not alive in the time of the second Temple, in which case we could have said that it refers to his return to the land [of promise]" (*Dis.* 32). A similar explanation is given to the Barayta about the resurrected who will not return to their dust (*Dis.* 25). However, it is not clear what the intention of the author is, when he tries to prove that certain sources should not be interpreted allegorically. The answer to this question might, perhaps, lie in the fact that the whole *Dissertation* is a compilation of several views which were expressed occasionally in the polemics about Maimonides' opinion on the Hereafter. This is how we can understand one stream of thought in the whole complex of the polemics, the aim of which was to justify Maimonides' opinion on the spiritual life of the Hereafter, and also his allegorical interpretation of the verses which are connected with the description of the Hereafter.[111] We have already shown (see above, p. 18) that the verse "yet the soul of my lord shall be bound in the bundle of life"[112] is explained by Maimonides in the *Guide of the Perplexed* as "the thing that remains of man after death." The *same* verse is given the *same* explanation in the *Dissertation* (32): "Since from the time [the soul] died it has gone to rest, so that it is bound in a bundle of life."[113] On the other hand, the author of the *Dissertation* is of the opinion that the soul is in need of a body in order to be resurrected, which again is a complete contrast to Maimonides' conception. Paragraphs 29–32 of the *Dissertation* lead us to the conclusion that the author interpreted the meaning of the Hereafter in the Mishnah "every Jew possesses a share in the Hereafter" as the Messianic era.

In the next paragraphs (*Dis.* 33–34) the author changes his mind, saying that "it is certain that the Hereafter which is taught in our Mishnah[114] is no other than the Hereafter [which comes] at the end, which cannot be reached by man unless through the resurrection of the dead" (*Dis.* 34). His exposition of the matter is very unclear, as though he were unable to reach any conclusion. The fact is that the author tries to adapt a certain interpretation of verses and mishnaic sources which in his view deal literally with the resurrection which will take place in the Messianic era. On the other hand, he is not sure if that interpretation is right: "And since we have explained that the literal meaning of the majority of those verses and the Mishnah concerning the resurrection of the dead refer only to the Messianic era, [it is clear that this is] also the [meaning of] the rest of the verses and the oral traditions which are *generally* concerned with the resurrection of the dead and the Hereafter, [and] we should connect them all, too, with the Messianic era. [However], how do we [know] about the resurrection of the dead in the Hereafter? It seems to us that in most of the instances in which the sages referred to the Hereafter, they certainly meant only the Hereafter [that will take place] at the end, after the Messianic era" (*Dis.* 33). It is obvious that the author does misquote the talmudic source in order to prove the validity of his assertion, as in the following quotation: "[Rava said, how do we know about resurrection from the Torah? Because it is written]: 'Let Reuben live' [means] in the Messianic era 'and not die'[115] [means] in the Hereafter" (*Dis.* 33). The talmudic text reads *ha-ʿolam ha-zeh* (this world) and *not* "the Messianic era."[116]

The author of the *Dissertation* draws a clear distinction between

the Messianic era and the Hereafter. The Hereafter must be preceded by bodily resurrection (*Dis.* 34) "because [this] world will be
destroyed during the interval [which will take place] between the
Messianic era and the Hereafter, as it is said [in the Gemara]: 'six
thousand years shall the world exist, and one [thousand years more]
it shall be desolate.'"[117] The concept that the Hereafter will be
another world, a future world after the destruction of this world, fits
in with the theory which is held by RAbaD (see above, p. 14) and is
contradicted by Maimonides in the *Guide of the Perplexed*[118] and in
Chapter Eight of *Hilkhot Teshuvah*. The author of the *Dissertation*
believes that every living creature in the world will be dead when the
world is destroyed. The next world will be the world of the Hereafter, but only those who are resurrected will have a share in it; thus,
he who denies the resurrection of the dead is punished for his denial
and will not be resurrected, and therefore will not possess a share in
the Hereafter (*Dis.* 34): "Therefore the sages said that 'he who
denies the resurrection of the dead has no share in the Hereafter,'[119] because the Hereafter is reached only through the resurrection of the dead, and he, having no share in the resurrection of the
dead because he denied it, will have no share in the Hereafter." The
author goes on to prove that the Mishnah of *Pereq Heleq* refers *not* to
the Messianic era *but* to the Hereafter, which Hereafter is the Day of
Judgment which follows the Messianic era (*Dis.* 35). The verse "they
shall inherit the land forever"[120] fits in well with the author's theory
that the righteous will sit in the Hereafter since they will have
bodies in it: ". . . it means that their 'sitting' [of the righteous] is not
in heaven but on earth. And since this is so, it was necessary to say
that they will live on earth forever."

The following paragraph (*Dis.* 36) introduces a sharp and new
turn from the arguments which were presented up to now. The *Dissertation* brings up Maimonides' statement which is an integral part
of his exposition in Chapter Eight of *Hilkhot Teshuvah*. The *Dissertation* reads: "However, it should be said that 'the good which is in
store for the righteous' in the Hereafter is called here 'inheriting the
land' by allegory" (*Dis.* 36). The author does not refer, even by a
hint, to Maimonides. Maimonides does not refer in Chapter Eight

to the biblical verse "they shall inherit the land forever," which appears at the beginning of the Mishnah "every Jew possesses a share in the Hereafter," etc. But he does expound some other verses which refer to the Hereafter allegorically. It seems that the author of the *Dissertation* is now revealing another aspect of the polemics, i.e., the vindication of Maimonides' opinion in Chapter Eight. He tries to interpret the term "resurrection of the dead" from a new point of view: "The teaching 'He who denies the resurrection of the dead' means a complete [denial] of the resurrection of the dead, that is to say, that he does not believe [at all] in the resurrection of the dead" (*Dis.* 36). What the author wants to say is that he who denies the resurrection denies it completely, whether the resurrection in the Messianic era or in the Hereafter. "We have explained above that those [verses] refer only to the Messianic era (the verses of Daniel), and he who adduces proof from them does not intend to adduce proof in regard to the resurrection of the dead which is taught in our Mishnah, in order to say that [those verses refer to the] resurrection of the dead and the Hereafter which are taught in our Mishnah. However, [it is obvious] that the sages referred only to those who assert that there is no hint at all in the Bible of the resurrection of the dead, neither in the Messianic era nor in the Hereafter. Therefore they adduced proof from those verses in order to show that there is at least a hint in the verses of the resurrection of the dead" (*Dis.* 36). In accordance with the above passage, the sages who discussed the matter in the Gemarah on the Mishnah of *Pereq Ḥeleq* wanted to adduce proof from biblical sources about the general belief in resurrection, as, for example, the verses from the Book of Daniel[121] which in fact, according to the interpretation in the *Dissertation,* point to the resurrection which will occur in the Messianic era. The author of the *Dissertation* is struggling with the material which he himself uses to prove and to disprove according to different opinions in the talmudic exegesis on the subject of *tehiyyat ha-metim* (resurrection of the dead). The author admits that it is difficult to find textual support from the Bible on resurrection, but on the other hand there are several verses which point to the Hereafter. This is the opinion held by the author of the *Treatise,* with the exception that the *Treatise* interprets the verses of Daniel as the only ones which point to bodily resurrection.[122] The author of the *Dissertation* holds that "the Hereafter, which is the Day of Judgment, will come only after the Messianic era" (*Dis.* 36). This view contradicts the beginning of the same paragraph, which maintains an idea identical with that expressed by Maimonides in Chapter Eight.

The next assertion in the *Dissertation* refers again to Maimonides' interpretation of the talmudic source on the absence of food in the Hereafter:[123] "And thus the subject of the Hereafter is explicitly explained by our teachers by saying . . . that 'there is no eating or drinking in the Hereafter.' It is well known that these instances refer only to the Hereafter, and they do not refer at all to the Messianic era since in that [era] eating and drinking will exist. From there you deduce that in the [Hereafter] resurrection of the dead will take place, as we have already explained several times. As it is said: 'Let Reuben live' [which means] in this world 'and not die' [which means] in the Hereafter" (*Dis.* 37). The last sentence, which is a quotation from the Talmud, does not define the words "live" or "die" in respect to "this world" (*ha-ʿolam ha-zeh*) or in respect to "the Hereafter" (*ha-ʿolam ha-ba*). It is possible to understand that the meaning of the life of Reuben in this world and in the Hereafter is the continuous life of one's soul as it is explained by Maimonides: ". . . that life comes to a man after the life in the [physical] world. . . "[124] In that connection the author, in *Dis.* 37, says: "From there you deduce that in the [Hereafter] resurrection of the dead will take place." This is a rather vague deduction because the author bases himself on the talmudic assertion which is also used as a main source by Maimonides, namely, "'there is no eating or drinking in the Hereafter.' It is well known that these instances refer only to the Hereafter . . ." (*Dis.* 37). Therefore, it is suggested that this paragraph, as well as the preceding paragraph (*Dis.* 36), belongs to *the school of the pro-Maimonideans,* which school sought a way to show that Maimonides *did believe* in the resurrection of the dead. The latter paragraphs suit the first part of the *Treatise,* which maintains that in the Hereafter there is spiritual existence only, but leaves room for an ambiguous interpretation of the term "resurrection of the dead."

Some more quotations from the Gemara on *Pereq Ḥeleq* which

have not yet been mentioned in the *Dissertation* are examined in paragraphs 38 and 39. The author alludes to verses which in his view point to the Messianic era and not to the Hereafter. This is how one should understand the words of Rabbi Yoḥanan: "All the prophets prophesied [only about the Messianic era]"[125] namely, on a specific and well-known subject (*Dis.* 38). This is also, according to the *Dissertation* the view of Ula,[126] who interpreted the verse "He will swallow up death forever"[127] as meaning "that the righteous who attain the Messianic era will not die, but they will pass from peace to peace—from the Messianic era to the life of the Hereafter" (*Dis.* 38). On the other hand, a different opinion is expressed by Samuel, who maintained: "This world differs from the Messianic era only in respect to the servitude of the kingdoms."[128] Therefore, it is asserted in *Dis.* 38, "death will exist in the Messianic era, for those who had not died before it, meaning that those will be lucky enough to live in that era. And we too, according to our humble opinion, accept the words of Samuel" (*Dis.* 38). This means that the author of the above-discussed paragraph is of the opinion of Maimonides about the meaning of the Messianic era "that the world goes its customary way,"[129] hence, resurrection of the dead *is not expected* during the historical time. As to the verse "He will swallow up death forever," it should be understood as the life of the Hereafter, which is really the opinion of Maimonides in Chapter Eight: "That good is a life which is free from death," etc. We must come to the conclusion that the latter part of the *Dissertation opposes the whole argument* of those paragraphs of the *Dissertation,* which motivation is: bodily resurrection during the Messianic era and in the Hereafter. Whereas the ideas which are discussed in the paragraphs which defend the theory of reward and punishment to the body and the soul together, an object which cannot be achieved without corporeal resurrection, suit the idea which is expressed at the end of the *Treatise on Resurrection,*[130] the ideas which are expressed in the last paragraphs of the *Dissertation* suit some of the main arguments in the *Treatise* about the spiritual existence in the Hereafter.[131] The last paragraphs of the *Dissertation* seem to harmonize with the opinions which are expressed by the *nasi* Sheshet,[132] who follows the system of Maimonides (see above, p. 45).

It seems that in order to conceal the sharp contradictions of opinions which exist between the various paragraphs of the *Dissertation,* the author goes back to remind the readers about the Barayta with which we have dealt in detail (*Dis.* 38): "The dead whom the Holy One, blessed be He, will resurrect in the Messianic era [will not revert to dust]."[133] The author stresses the fact that the wording of the text is very precise: "The dead . . . and *not* the righteous . . . [will be resurrected]." By that he hints at the previous discussion, which maintains that corporeal resurrection will precede the Hereafter. However, one may wonder how far the author goes in order to camouflage the real meaning of the ideas which are dealt with in the same paragraph. We mean that he had to change the text of the Barayta which he used as proof for bodily resurrection. The original text of the Barayta, as it stands in the Babylonian Talmud, *Sanhedrin* 92a, reads explicitly: "The righteous whom God will resurrect will not revert to their dust," which contradicts entirely not only the author's quotation but also his interpretation.

The following quotations from Tractate *Sanhedrin,* which compare the Hereafter to "the wine that has been kept maturing . . . because there is nothing in the world which gladdens one's heart like wine . . ." (*Dis.* 39), add to and emphasize the previous conclusion that the author follows the opinion of Maimonides on the Hereafter. "Thereafter," says the author of the *Dissertation,* "it is compared to wine because the joy [will reach] the highest possible degree of joy. And what is the significance of 'kept maturing in its grapes'? To tell you that this joy has [never] been tested by man in [this] world, like wine which has been kept maturing in its grapes, untouched by any hand" (*Dis.* 39). This is the meaning, according to the *Dissertation,* of the talmudic exegesis: "All the prophets prophesied only about the Messianic era, but as for the Hereafter 'the eye hath not seen, O Lord, beside thee.'"[134] A similar explanation is given in *Mishneh Torah:*[135] "It is not in the capacity of man to understand the complete [meaning] of the good of the Hereafter; nobody except God Himself knows its greatness, its beauty . . . God made it for him who waits for Him. . . . 'All the good things about which the prophets prophesied' to Israel are limited to material delights [which will take place] in the Messianic era, etc. All the prophets without exception prophesied (*kol ha-nevi'im kullam*)[136] about the

Messianic era only, but [as for] the Hereafter 'the eye hath not seen, O Lord, beside thee.'"[137]

The end of the *Dissertation* leaves the reader with an unsolved problem. What do the sources really mean to tell us about the eschatological eon? "And there are instances in which the [term] 'the Hereafter' refers to the Messianic era" (*Dis.* 40), otherwise we will have to say that the sages admitted "that there is eating and drinking in the Hereafter." "These problems cannot be solved because they are so remote from [any possible] solution. However, they should be interpreted in connection with the Messianic era, in which eating and drinking exist." Samuel, who maintains that there is no difference between this world and the Messianic era, will not accept as valid the Barayta which describes the enormous quantity of the wine[138] that each grape will produce in the Hereafter, which Hereafter probably means, here, the Messianic era.

The author sums up the problem and leaves it without solution: ". . . wherever you find any reference [in the talmudic sources] to the Hereafter, in which it is proved that eating and drinking exist there—if it is a matter which can be interpreted, it should be interpreted, but if not—it is clear that it refers only to the Messianic era" (*Dis.* 40). This semi-solution of the meaning of the term "Hereafter" in the talmudic sources gives the true reflection of the description of the subject in those sources.

Nevertheless, the author states that "after having explained the subject of the Hereafter which is taught in our Mishnah ('Every Jew possesses a share in the Hereafter'), according to its literal meaning and according to the tradition that was handed down to us by our fathers and our teachers, and according to the widespread tradition accepted by all Jews, as well as according to reason and according to justice, as it seems in our humble opinion, we resume our explanation of the rest of the Mishnah along the usual lines" (*Dis.* 40). This is how the author combines all the possible components of the arguments on the subject of our *Dissertation on Resurrection and Hereafter*. In his last statement the author admits that the whole discussion up till then had gone beyond the bounds of the usual Commentary of the Mishnah, and that it was dedicated to the subject of the Hereafter which is taught in our Mishnah in *Pereq Ḥeleq*.

Conclusion

The text which appears to be a part of the Commentary on *Pereq Ḥeleq* of Tractate *Sanhedrin* is a separate *Dissertation*. This *Dissertation* was probably composed by a group of Jewish scholars who took part in the polemics which arose around Maimonides' explicit opinion on the Hereafter and implicit opinion on resurrection. The above-analyzed text could also be a compilation of different sources which are connected with the polemics. The internal order of the paragraphs does not add clarity to the subject. Our examination shows that several contradictory opinions are brought together and form a compilation which, perhaps, preceded the composition of the *Treatise on Resurrection*. It seems that the *Treatise on Resurrection,* as well as some of the other units of literature which are edited here, was written late in the first half of the thirteenth century or even later than that. The earliest units of the text are those of the letter of Rabbi Meir ben Todros Abulafia, while the latest units are those of the *Treatise on Resurrection*. The *Dissertation,* which was inserted in the Commentary of the book *Yad Ramah,* perhaps for editorial reasons only, furnishes us with the main ideas of the *Treatise on Ressurrection,* its background and its motives.

I think it advisable to sum up here the main ideas of the *Dissertation*.

The first part of the *Dissertation* (Pars. 1–10) deals with the following points:

1. The first sentence of the Mishnah of *Pereq Ḥeleq* states that every Jew possesses a share in the Hereafter.

2. The belief in the Hereafter is an article of faith in the Torah of Moses and cannot be questioned.

3. The Hereafter comes after the Messianic era. It is also the Day of Judgment, and reward and punishment will take place then. Judgment will be meted out to the body and the soul together.

4. Resurrection of the bodies will take place in the Hereafter.

5. The talmudic statement that there is no food in the Hereafter should be understood literally: there will nevertheless be a corporeal existence.

The second part of the *Dissertation* (pars. 11–18) deals with the following points:

1. Some contemporaries maintain that resurrection will take place during the Messianic era. The resurrected will then die again. This is also the opinion of Maimonides.

2. The first letter to Lunel and also the second were written in order to disprove Maimonides' idea, in Chapter Eight, that there is no corporeal existence in the Hereafter.

3. The reasons for, and the events which preceded, the composition of the *Treatise on Resurrection*.

4. A long quotation from the *Treatise on Resurrection*.

The third part of the *Dissertation* (pars. 19–40) deals with the following points:

1. The question of corporeal existance in the Hereafter.

2. A detailed study of a Barayta stating that God will resurrect the dead.

3. The claim that the Mishnah on *Pereq Ḥeleq* refers to the Messianic era.

4. The claim that it refers to the Hereafter.

5. Maimonides, Chapter Eight, *Hilkhot Teshuvah,* is quoted.

6. The term "resurrection of the dead" is nowhere defined and is implicitly understood as the immortality of the soul.

7. The Messianic era will not be one of miracles or resurrection.

8. The meaning of the term "Hereafter" changes according to the various talmudic sources.

Notes

1. On the sequence of these chapters in the Mishnah *Sanhedrin*, see J.N. Epstein, *Mavo*, vol. 2, p. 997.

2. On the difference among the versions, see Rabinovitz, *Diqduqei Sofrim*, vol. 9 (*Sanhedrin*), p. 247; *Be'er Sheva'*, p. 10b; W. H. Lowe, *The Mishnah*, p. 128; R. Margaliot, *Sinai*, vol. 10, p. 185.

3. Doubts about Meir Abulafia's authorship of the Commentary on *Sanhedrin* must arise from the remarks made by Rabinovitz, *Diqduqei Sofrim*, vol. 9, pp. 6 and 130b, n. 30. See also: J. N. Epstein, *Tarbiz*, vol. 4, pp. 20 ff.; H. Merhawyah, *Tarbiz*, vol. 33, pp. 259–86, and vol. 35, p. 278.

4. See the reproduction of the title page in the Appendix.

5. *B. Sanhedrin* 99a, Avot 3:15.

6. The whole anecdote is quoted in Paragraph 5 of the *Dissertation*.

7. *J. Peah*, ch. 2, halakha 6 reads: "Rabbi Zeira on the authority of Samuel said: It is not to be deduced from the rules (halakhot), nor from talmudic exegesis (haggadot), or from the talmudic additions (tosafot), but only from the Talmud itself (namely, from the decisions of the Amoraim)." See also RaShbaM to *B. Baba Batra*, 130b: 'Ad she-y'omru lo halakha le-ma'ase. These quotations demonstrate the talmudic approach to *haggadah*.

8. *B. Sanhedrin* 64b, 90b.

9. Num. 15:31.

10. Ps. 84:5.

11. *B. Sanhedrin* 64b, 90b; *Makkot* 11; *Berakhot* 26.

12. *M.T. Hilkhot Teshuvah* 8.

13. *B. Berakhot* 17a.

14. *M.T. Hilkhot Teshuvah* 8, *Hassagot RAbaD*.

15. Dan. 12:2.

16. Ps. 50:2.

17. *B. Sanhedrin* 91a. See our quotation in par. 5 of the *Dissertation*.

18. There are two versions of the same chapter. See W. Bacher, "Die zweite Version von Saadja's Abschnitt . . . ," p. 219. H. Malter, *Saadia Gaon*, p. 363, mentions an "anonymous paraphrase" in Hebrew of the *Book of Beliefs and Opinions*, which contains chapter 7 "of Saadia's work . . . but with considerable changes . . ." Without going into further details, we must point out that the chapter on resurrection in Saadiah's work is in itself problematic.

19. Saadiah Gaon, *Sefer ha-'Emunot*, chap. 9, p. 134.

20. *B. Sanhedrin* 91a.

21. The reply is quoted in *ʾArugat ha-Bosem*, vol. 4, p. 256.

22. M. Abulafia, *Kitāb*, p. 14.

23. *Treatise* 9, 10.

24. *B. Shabbat* 77a: "Out of all that God created in His world there is not one thing that is in vain."

25. *Treatise* 23, 24.

26. *Treatise* 52.

27. Moses ben Maimon, *Pereq Ḥeleq*, ed. Holzer, p. 139.

28. *Treatise*, 23.

29. *Treatise* 16.

30. *Treatise* 16.

31. *Treatise* 30.

32. *M.T. Book of Judges, Kings* 11:3.

33. Ibid. 12.

34. M. Abulafia, *Kitāb*, p. 14.

35. Lam. 1:12.

36. Deut. 22:7.

37. 1 Kings 19:8.

38. Sheshet, *Nusaḥ ha-ʾIggeret*, p. 413.

39. *Treatise* 52.

40. *Treatise* 10.

41. *Treatise* 9.

42. Meir Abulafia, 1180–1244. E. E. Urbach maintains that Abulafia wrote to Lunel in 1202. *Zion*, vol. 12, p. 150. A quite different version of the same letter is quoted in Abraham ben Azriel, *ʿArugat ha-Bosem*, vol. 2 p. 259. *ʿArugat ha-Bosem* was written about 1234. See also J. N. Epstein, *Tarbiz*, vol. 4 p. 23, n. 47.

43. Saadiah Gaon, *Sefer ha-ʾEmunot*, chap. 7, p. 116: chap. 9, p. 136.

44. Sheshet, *Nusaḥ ha-ʾIggeret*, p. 419.

45. J. L. Teicher, *Melilah*, vol. 1, p. 82.

46. M. Abulafia, *Kitāb*, p. 50.

47. *Treatise* 17.

48. *Treatise* 16.

49. *Treatise* 30.

50. *M.T. Book of Judges, Hilkhot Melakhim* 11.

51. *Treatise* 16, 20.

52. Bodleian MS no. 2493[3] of the *Treatise on Resurrection* includes a preface which mentions the problem of the Arabic-Hebrew translations.

53. In the preface of the Bodleian MS no. 2493[3], for instance, the names of al-Ḥarizi and Joseph ben Joel are mentioned as the translators into Hebrew and Arabic.

54. We refer in this work to the Hebrew and Arabic texts which were edited by J. Finkel.

55. D. H. Baneth assumes that there exist three translations in addition to the

Arabic original: the Hebrew translation by Ibn Tibbon, an Arabic translation from the text of Ibn Tibbon by Joseph ben Joel, and another translation by al-Ḥarizi from the Arabic of Joseph ben Joel. *Tarbiz*, vol. 11 (1940), pp. 260 ff. See also D. H. Baneth, *Tarbiz*, vol. 13 (1942), pp. 37 ff.; J. L. Teicher, *Melilah*, vol. 1 (1944), pp. 88 ff.

56. *Treatise* 1–14.

57. Dan. 12:2.

58. Ibid. 13.

59. *Treatise* 21.

60. *Treatise* 22.

61. *Treatise* 21.

62. Ibid.

63. Moses ben Maimon, *Einleitung* . . ., ed. Holzer, p. 16, n. 149.

64. *Treatise* 21.

65. Azariah Rossi, *Me'or*, p. 92.

66. *Treatise* 22.

67. Azariah Rossi, *Me'or*, p. 92.

68. E. Pocock, *Notae*, p. 87, has: "The thirteenth principle is the resurrection of the dead and we have already explained its content and its reasoning (*ʿinyano ve sodotav*)." The words "content" and "reasoning" are in addition to the standard text of the Introduction to the Commentary on *Pereq Ḥeleq*. The Cambridge MS, R.S. 26 (2) has: ". . . and we have already explained its reasoning (*sodotav*)."

69. J. N. Epstein, *Tarbiz*, vol. 4, p. 23, n. 47; Taubes, *Oẓar*, p. 484.

70. *Treatise* 23.

71. *Treatise* 24.

72. Ibid.

73. Ibid.

74. *B. Berakhot* 17a.

75. *Treatise* 24.

76. Sheshet, *Nusaḥ ha-ʾIggeret*, p. 426.

77. M. Abulafia, *Kitāb*, p. 14.

78. *Treatise* 26.

79. *M.T. Book of Judges, Hilkhot Melakhim* 11.

80. *Treatise* 30.

81. Ibid.

82. *M.T. Book of Judges, Hilkhot Melakhim* 11. The text of the standard printed editions of the above chapter deviates greatly from the Rome edition, 1480, which includes many pre-censored passages. Cf. Cambridge MS Add. 1564, probably from the thirteenth century. It is evident that this text underwent changes at several hands. See also Schiller-Szinessy, *Jewish Chronicle*, vol. 17 3 July, 1885, p. 6. See L.N. Goldfeld, *Hilkhot Melakhim u-Milḥamot ve-Melekh ha-Mashiaḥ, Sinai*, year 49, vol. 96, a-b, 1984.

83. M. Abulafia, *Kitāb*, pp. 14 ff., 50ff.

84. *B. Berakhot* 17a.

85. *B. Sanhedrin* 91a.

86. *M.T. Book of Knowledge, Hilkhot Teshuvah* 8:2–3.

87. *B. B. Berakhot* 17a.

88. The text has *Rav*. Moses ben Maimon (RaMbaM, Maimonides) is not mentioned in a direct connection with the quotations from the *Treatise* in the *Dissertation*. The *only* instance in which his name is mentioned is *Dis.* 11. However, it is suggested in *Dis.* 14 that *Rav* stands for Maimonides: "they . . . adduced proof . . . from . . . Maimonides . . . [therefore] the people . . . were compelled to ask the Rabbi."

89. *B. Sanhedrin* 92a; *Seder Eliyahu*, ed. Friedmann, pp. 46, 164.

90. *Treatise* 22.

91. *B. Sanhedrin* 92a reads: "The righteous who . . . resurrect will not revert to . . ."

92. Cambridge, Genizah MS T-S K27, no. 6. This MS, which was published by me in *Kobez al Yad*, includes some interesting passages which may also have some bearing on the polemics. Fol. 8 of the MS brings proof of the resurrection of the righteous from the same Barayta.

93. Dan. 12:2.

94. Ibid. 9.

95. *Treatise* 46.

96. Ibid.

97. *Treatise* 47.

98. *Guide* III:37.

99. Exod. 13:17.

100. J. L. Teicher, *Melilah*, vol. 1, p. 87.

101. The text has "dead" instead of "righteous."

102. *Treatise* 23.

103. *B. Sanhedrin* 92a.

104. Isa. 60:21.

105. Dan. 12:3.

106. Isa. 66:24.

107. *Treatise* 23.

108. *M.T. Book of Knowledge, Hilkhot Teshuvah* 8.

109. Ibid. 3:6.

110. *Treatise* 22.

111. *M.T. Book of Knowledge, Hilkhot Teshuvah* 8.

112. 1 Sam. 25:29.

113. See also M. Vogelman, *Beit Mordekhai*, pp. 33 ff., about the use of this verse in rabbinic literature.

114. *B. Sanhedrin* 90a.

115. Deut. 33:6.

116. *B. Sanhedrin* 92a.

117. Ibid. 92b.

118. *Guide* II:29.

119. *B. Sanhedrin* 90a.

120. Isa. 60:21.

121. *B. Sanhedrin* 92a.

122. *Treatise* 6, 22, 38.

123. *B. Berakhot* 17a.

124. M.T. Book of Knowledge, *Hilkhot Teshuvah* 8.

125. *B. Sanhedrin* 99a.

126. *B. Sanhedrin* 91b.

127. Isa. 35:6.

128. *B. Sanhedrin* 99a.

129. *M.T. Hilkhot Melakhim* 12:1.

130. *Treatise* 52.

131. *Treatise* 24.

132. Sheshet, *Nusah ha-ʾIggeret.*

133. *B. Sanhedrin* 92a.

134. Ps. 31:9.

135. *M.T. Book of Knowledge, Repentance* 8:7.

136. Does the emphasis on *Kol-kullam* mean that the verses of Daniel are also included? *B. Sanhedrin* 99a reads only: "All the prophets . . . "

137. Ps. 31:9.

138. *B. Ketubbot* 111b.

Historical Background and Epilogue

The importance of establishing the authorship of the *Treatise* lies in the fact that it reflects one of the major subjects of conflict between two different conceptions of Jewish theology in the twelfth and thirteenth centuries. The actual conflict did not begin with the objection of RAbaD to Maimonides' opinion on the Hereafter as expressed in the *Book of Knowledge,* but with Rabbi Meir Abulafia's letter to Lunel, at the beginning of the thirteenth century.

The exponents of the opposing conceptions became involved in a bitter controversy lasting about one hundred years.[1] M. Steinschneider asserts that this controversy was one of the most important episodes in the history of the Jewish nation and religion.[2]

It seems that in the thirteenth century, Jewish orthodoxy was gradually becoming more sympathetic with the tenets of Christianity. Jewish orthodoxy followed the literal meaning of the biblical verses as well as the literal meaning of the Aggadah and fought against philosophy. This "hundred years war" took a new turn when the orthodox current of Judaism joined the Christian authorities in combatting the "heretical" opposition, namely, the philosophers. The result of the coalition between the opponents of Maimonides, and the Catholic Inquisition, was the public burning of the *Book of Knowledge* and the *Guide of the Perplexed,* once in Montpellier by the Franciscans in 1234, and again in Paris by the Dominicans in 1242.[3] This was followed by the burning of the Talmud in Paris.[4]

J. L. Teicher[5] makes the point that the causes of the spiritual conflict among the Jewish communities in France in the first half of the thirteenth century were the attacks against Maimonides' *Book of Knowledge* and the *Guide of the Perplexed.* The internal Jewish dispute on resurrection reflected the beliefs of the Christian world. It seems that to be heretics for the denial of physical resurrection would have

135

caused far-reaching changes in the status of the Jews, and would have deprived them of their privileges. Therefore, the minority of Jews who disputed physical resurrection had to accept this basic Christian doctrine. Maimonides' authority was already established in the Jewish communities of France. It seems that the burning of his books might even have brought about a ban on the whole of his *Mishneh Torah,* a danger of which his followers were probably aware. One way to clear themselves of the accusation of heresy was to compose the *Treatise on Resurrection.*

The Catholic Inquisition, which began its inquiries concerning heresy (by the appointment of Pope Gregory IX), would not have joined the Jewish leaders of Montpellier, who opposed Maimonides and wished to ban his works, without having ample evidence that certain Maimonidean opinions meant heresy from the Christian point of view. The interests of both parties, the Jewish and the Christian, were combined for a common aim.[6]

Bishop Guillaume d'Auvergne of Paris, who was instrumental the auto-da-fé of the Talmud,[7] accuses all Jews living in Moslem countries of heresy against Jewish Law because of the influence of Moslem-Greek philosophy. He criticizes Maimonides indirectly in connection with certain aspects of the Aristotelian philosophy.[8] It seems almost certain that Guillaume d'Auvergne took part in the inquiry of the Inquisition into possible heresy in the works of Maimonides, as part of the same inquiry which followed the accusations made by adversaries of Maimonides in Montpellier. It was perhaps then, at the time of the burning of the books of Maimonides, that a papal decree against the *Book of Knowledge* and the *Guide of the Perplexed* was issued.[9] The inquiry into heresy included matters which proved that the heretics rejected basic principles of belief that were accepted by both Christian and Jewish theologians.[10] One of the beliefs common to Christians and to Jews under Christian influence was the belief in bodily resurrection. This belief seems to have been taken for granted after the Novella of Justinian (see above, p. 5). Although no direct indication of this is given by the sources which mention the condemnation of Maimonides' *Book of Knowledge* and the *Guide of the Perplexed,* it seems, by implication, that one of the reasons for the burning of those works was the total rejection of bodily resurrectioni in the *Book of Knowledge.*

The composition of the *Treatise* was an answer to the anti-Maimonidean movement, a movement which threatened Maimonides' halakhic and philosophic authority. The authority of Maimonides was already deeply rooted among the Eastern Jewish communities and gradually penetrated the Jewish Ashkenazi communities until it reached Spain, Maimonides' homeland. The *Treatise* cleared Maimonides' position on the belief in bodily resurrection. This is, perhaps, the reason why, following the publishing of the *Treatise on Resurrection,* the *Book of Knowledge* is not mentioned any more in the sources which deal again with the heretical implications of the *Guide of the Perplexed.* It was not until Maimonides was cleared of heresy by a papal decree that the *Guide of the Perplexed* was safe. A Genizah document which was written by a pro-Maimonidean Italian Jew reveals some interesting details in this matter.[11] It is a Hebrew letter addressed to the *nagid* (head of community) David, the grandson of Maimonides, in Egypt. A passage of particular interest reads:[12] "In the month of Tamuz (no year is given) . . . God stirred up the spirit of the higher Bishop, the father of all the bishops, and he [the Pope] had a proclamation [read] in the Synagogue [of Rome], may it stand forever, and he also had it [the proclamation] written down, saying: 'So said the high Bishop: . . . I was given by God the rule and the power . . . and He appointed me to be the *hegmon* (Pope?) over all the people so that I shall be able to forbid . . . and to restrain . . . And my mind aroused me to deal with the books of the Rabbi, [Rabbi] Moses of righteous and blessed memory, and with the book *Moreh Nevukhim* (the *Guide of the Perplexed*) . . .'" The Pope expresses his appreciation of the *Guide* by several phrases in rhymed prose and then he goes on: "Therefore any intelligent person who wants to know God should always consult the book called the *Guide,* because it is the basis of the Law and the reason for piety. Because it destroys that which those who believe in the eternity of the world have built, with the help of valid proofs, and it builds the fortifications of strengthening the [theory of the] creation of the world by *other* proofs. And although there are *hints in his opinions* which point toward a *rejection of our belief,* [these hints] are not too palpable, because he told them [in advance] that he was a Jew." The Pope goes on to threaten any critic of the *Guide* with a fine of one hundred silver pieces. The letter also mentions

that the two Italian Jews who went to the Pope's court to get his proclamation were able to obtain the *haskamah ha-qadmonah ha-yedu ʿah*
(the earlier known decree), which, as it seems, was a previous papal
decree against Maimonides' works, and thus to annul its validity. It
might well be[13] that the above-mentioned decree was the one which
was signed by the Pope as a result of the investigations of the Inquisition and the intervention of the Jewish leaders of Montpellier,
events which had led to the burning of the *Book of Knowledge* and the
Guide of the Perplexed about fifty years earlier.

The document includes important details about other facets of
the controversy which took place approximately in the last decade of
the thirteenth century. At that time it was probably Pope Nicholas
IV (1288–92) who exonerated Maimonides from heresy in a very
honorable and clear proclamation which did not leave any doubts
about the papal attitude towards Maimonides' works. The exonera-
tion is of the *Guide of the Perplexed* and *not* of the *Book of Knowledge*,[14]
which was probably also among the books that the Pope was
acquainted with, since he says in the above document "the books of
the Rabbi."

Near the middle of the "hundred years war" about Maimonides'
philosophical and theological ideas, and perhaps after the auto-da-
fé of the *Book of Knowledge* and the *Guide of the Perplexed*, we think, the
pro-Maimonidean party in Judaism brought out the *Treatise on
Resurrection, Ma'amar Teḥiyyat ha-Metim*, a composition which cleared
Maimonides from heresy as to the belief in resurrection.

Notes

1. The ban of Solomon Adret ben Abraham, 1306, against the philosophical
work of Maimonides brings this episode in Jewish history to its end. RaShbA,
She'elot, vol. 1, no. 418.

2. M. Steinschneider, *Oẓar neḥmad*, vol. 2 p. 230.

3. Hillel ben Samuel of Verona (d. ca. 1291) describes the events in his *ʾIggeret*,
p. 71.

4. I. F. Baer, *A History of Jews*, p. 484, n. 60.

5. J. L. Teicher, "Christian Theology," *Journal of Theological Studies*, vol. 43, p.
69.

6. Ibid., p. 70.

7. J. Gutmann, *Thomas von Aquino,* p. 32, n. 1, asserts that Guillaume d'Auvergne used the Latin translation of the *Guide* (probably from the Hebrew translation of al-Ḥarizi). Idem, "Der Einfluss," 141.

8. J. Gutmann, "Der Einfluss," p. 146, n. 2, has a quotation from the Latin of Guillaume d'Auvergne.

9. J. Mann, *Texts and Studies,* vol. 1, p. 423.

10. I. F. Baer, *Studien,* pp. 63–64; idem, *Tarbiz,* vol. 2, p. 172.

11. A. E. Harkavy, *Haqedem,* vol. 3 (1912), pp. 111–14.

12. Ibid., p. 112. See also E. Strauss, *Toldot ha-Yehudim,* vol. 1, p. 133.

13. J. Mann, *Texts and Studies,* vol. 1, p. 423.

14. On the Latin translation of the *Guide,* see: Z. Graetz, *Divrei,* vol. 5 p. 62; J. L. Teicher, "Christian Theology," *Journal of Theological Studies,* vol. 43 p. 71; idem, "Latin-Hebrew School," *Homenaje a Millas-Vallicrosa,* vol. 2 p. 441, n. 40.

Bibliography

Abraham ben Nathan ha-Yarḥi. "Commentary on *Kallah Rabbati.*" Edited by M. Higger. *Jewish Quarterly Review,* V. 24 (1934), 331–348.

Albo, J. *Sefer ha-ʿIqqarim.* Translated by I. Husik. 4 vols. Philadelphia, 1930.

Al-Ghazālī. *Tahāfut al-falāsifah* [Incoherence of the philosophers]. Lahore, 1958.

Authorized Daily Prayer Book, Translated by S. Singer. London, 1962.

Averroes. *Kitāb faṣl-al-maqāl.* Edited by M. J. Mueller. Munich, 1859.

———. *Tahāfut al-tahāfut.* Translated by S. Van den Bergh. Vol. 1, Oxford, 1954.

Bacher, W. "Die zweite Version von Saadja's Abschnitt ueber die Wiederbelebung der Todten." In *Fetschrift zum 80 Geburtstage Moritz Steinschneiders'.* Leipzig, 1896, pp. 219–226; 98–112 (Heb. section).

Baer, I. F. *Studien zur Geschichte der Juden in Aragonien.* Berlin, 1913.

Baron, S. W. *A Social and Religious History of the Jews.* Vols. 5 and 8. New York, 1957, 1958.

Dienstag, Jacob I., ed. *Eschatology in Maimonidean Thought.* New York: KTAV, 1983.

Finkel, J. "Maimonides' *Treatise on Resurrection.*" *PAAJR,* Vol. 9 (1939).

Guttmann, Jacob. "Der Einfluss der maimonidischen Philosophie auf das christlische Abendland." In W. Bacher, *Moses ben Maimon, sein Leben, Werke und sein Einfluss,* vol. 1, Leipzig, 1908, pp. 135–220.

———. *Das Verhaeltniss des Thomas von Aquino zum Judentum und zur juedischen Litteratur.* Goettingen, 1891.

Guttmann, Julius. *Philosophies of Judaism.* New York, 1964.

Harkavy, A. E. "Fragment einer Apologie des Maimonidischen Ma'amar Teḥiyyat ha-Metim." *Zeitschrift fuer Hebraeische Bibliographie,* vol. 2 (1897), pp. 125–128; 181–188.

Hyman, A. "Maimonides' Thirteen Principles." Edited by A. Altmann, *Jewish Mediaeval and Renaissance Studies.* Cambridge, Mass., 1967, pp. 119–144.

Ibn Abī Uṣaybiʿa, *ʿUyūn al-anbāʾ, fī ṭabaqāt al-aṭibbāʾ.* Edited by Dr. Wizā Riḍā, Beirut, 1965.

Ibn Khallikān, *Wafayāt al-Aʿyān,* Vol. 2, Cairo, 1310, [1894].

Jastrow, H. A. *Dictionary of the Targumim.* 2 parts in 1 vol. London, 1903.

Josephus Flavius. *Jewish Antiquities,* Vol. 18 New York: Loeb Classical Library, 1965.

Kahle, P. H. *The Cairo Geniza.* Oxford, 1959.

Malter, H. *Saadia Gaon: His Life and Works.* Philadelphia, 1921.

Mann, J. *Texts and Studies.* Vol. 1, Cincinnati, 1931.

Marxsen, W. *The Resurrection of Jesus of Nazareth.* London, 1970.

Moses ben Maimon. *Mose Maimuni's "Einleitung zu* Chelek." *Im arabischen Urtext und in der hebraeischen Uebersetzung.* Edited by J. Holzer, Berlin, 1901.

———. Maimonides Commentarius in Mischnam E codicibus Hunt. 117 et Pococke 295 in Bibliothecae Bodleiana Oxoniensi servatis et 72–73 Bibliotheca Sassoonienis Letchworth. Edited by R. Edelman. Hafniae: Sumptibus E. Munksgaard, 3 vols., 1956–66.

———. *The Guide of the Perplexed.* Translated by S. Pines. Chicago, 1963.

———. *Ma'amar Tehiyyat ha-Metim. Maimonides' Treatise on Resurrection (Maqāla fī Tehiyyat ha-Metim).* The original Arabic and Samuel ibn Tibbon's Hebrew translation and glossary. Edited, with critical apparatus, by J. Finkel. New York: PAAJR, 1939.

Pocock, E. *Notae Miscellanae Philologico-Biblicae quibus Porta Mosis, sive praefationum R. Mosis Maimonides in libros Mischnajoth Commentaris praemissarium* . . . Leipzig, 1705.

Poznanski, S. *Babylonische Geonim im nachgaonaeischen Zeitalter.* Berlin, 1914.

Sheshet ha-Nasi ben Isaac. "Nusaḥ ha-Iggeret shekatav he-Ḥakham ha-Nasi Rabbi Sheshet Zvi le-Ḥakhmei Lunel." Edited by A. Marx. *Jewish Quarterly Review,* n.s. vol. 25 (1935).

Sonne, I. "A Scrutiny of the Charges of Forgery against Maimonides' *Letter on Resurrection." Proceedings of the American Academy for Jewish Research.* vol. 21 (1952).

Steinschneider, M. *Hebraeische Uebersetzungen des Mittealters und die Juden als Dolmetscher.* Berlin, 1893.

Talmud. *The Babylonian Talmud.* Translated into English . . . under the editorship of I. Epstein, London, 1961.

Teicher, J. L. "Christian Theology and the Jewish Opposition to Maimonides." *Journal of Theological Studies,* vol. 43 (1942), 68–76.

———. "Latin-Hebrew School of Translators in Spain in the Twelfth Century." In *Homenaje a Millás-Vallicrosa,* vol. 2, Barcelona, 1956, pp. 403–444.

———. "Maimonides' Letter to Joseph b. Jehudah: A Literary Forgery." *Journal of Jewish Studies,* vol. 1, no. 1 (1948–49), 35–54.

ר' אברהם בן ר' דוד (ראב"ד). השגות על משנה תורה להרמב"ם (ברוב ההוצאות).

ר' אברהם בן הרמב"ם. מלחמות השם. בעריכת ד. מרגליות. ירושלים: מוסד הרב קוק, תשי"ג/1953.

ר' אברהם בן ר' עזריאל. ערוגת הבושם. בעריכת א.א. אורבאך. 4 כרכים. ירושלים: "מקיצי נרדמים", תרצ"ט־תשכ"ג.

אבולעאפיא, ר'מאיר הלוי. כתאב אלרסאייל. פאריס, תרל"א/1871 (דפוס צלום: ירושלים, תשל"א).

————. יד רמ"ה על מסכת סנהדרין, תקנ"ח/1798; ורשה, תרנ"ה (צלום מזה: ניו־יורק, תשי"ג).

אברבנאל, דון יצחק. נחלת אבות על פרקי אבות. ויניציאה, שכ"ז/1567.

אדרת, ר' שלמה ז'. שאלות ותשובות הרשב"א; חלק ג', בני ברק, תש"ח/1948.

אורבאך, א.א. עמדתם של חכמי אשכנז וצרפת בפולמוס על הרמב"ם וספריו. ציון, 12 (תש"ז), 149־159.

אייזנבורג, ר' יששכר בער: ס' באר שבע. ויניציאה, שע"ד/1614.

אפשטיין, י.נ. מבוא לנוסח המשנה. ירושלים: הוצאת מאגנס, תש"ח/1948; צלום, שם, תשכ"ד/1964.

————. פירושי הריב"ן ופירושי וורמיזא. תרביץ, 4 (תרצ"ג), 11־34; 153 ,192; 295־296.

אשתור (שטרוס), א. תולדות היהודים במצרים וסוריא תחת שלטון המלכים. כרך א'. ירושלים: מוסד הרב קוק, תש"ד/1944.

בן־יהודה, אליעזר. מלון הלשון העברית. ירושלים, 1948.

בענט, ד. צ.: ר' יהודה אלחריזי ושלשלת התרגומים של מאמר תחיית המתים. תרביץ, 11 (ת"ש/1940), 260־270.

————. לנוסח מאמר תחיית המתים של הרמב"ם ולתרגומו. תרביץ, (13), (תש"ב/1942), 37־42.

בער, יצחק: לפרשת הויכוחים של יחיאל מפאריס ושל ר' משה בן נחמן. תרביץ, 2 (תרצ"א/1931), 172־187.

————. ישראל בעמים. ירושלים, 1955.

————. תולדות היהודים בספרד הנוצרית. ירושלים, 1959.

ברון, ש.: מחקרי יהדות אנגליה. התקופה, 30־31 (1946), 823־827.

גולדפלד, לאה נעמי, הלכות מלכים ומלחמות ומלך המשיח, סיני, שנה מ"ט, כרך צו, א־ב, תשמ"ה, סז־עט.

גרייץ, צבי: דברי ימי ישראל, כרך 5, ורשה, תרס"ח.

דינסטאג, י.י.: מאמר תחיית המתים; ביבליוגראפיה . . . קרית ספר, 48 (1973), 730, 740־.

הרכבי, א.א.: חדשים גם ישנים. הקדם, 3 (1912), 111־114; נדפס שוב בספרו "חדשים גם ישנים". ירושלים: כרמיאל, תש"ל, עמ' 443־446.

חננאל בן חושיאל: מגדל חננאל. ברלין, 1876.

טויבש, ח"צ: אוצר הגאונים למסכת סנהדרין. ירושלים, תשכ"ו/1966.

טייכר, י.ל.: זיוף ספרותי במאה הי"ג — מאמר תחיית המתים של הרמב"ם. מלילה, א (תש"ד/1944), 81־92.

ילין, ד.: מקור הקדמת כתאב אלרסאייל לרבי מאיר בן טודרוס הלוי. **קרית ספר**, 6 (1929), 139-144.

מירסקי, ש.ק.: הרמב"ם ויחסו אל הפשט והדרש. ב"הרמב"ם" בעריכת ש.ש. פדרבוש. ניו-יורק, 1956, עמ' 77-84.

מרגליות, ראובן: להקדמת הרמב"ם למשנה. **סיני**, 10 (תש"ב), קפג-קצא.

מרחביה, ח.: לשאלת רש"י לפרק "חלק". **תרביץ**, 33 (תשכ"ד), 259-286.

מרחביה, ח.: עוד לשאלת רש"י לפרק "חלק", **תרביץ** 35 (תשכ"ו) 278-294.

ר' משה בן מימון: משנה עם פרוש הרמב"ם; סדר נזיקין. תרגום עברי מאת י. קאפח. ירושלים: מוסד הרב קוק, תשכ"ד/1964.

———. משניות עם פירוש הרמב"ם. נפולי, רנ"ב/1492 (צלום: ירושלים, תש"ל/1970).

———. פירוש הרמב"ם למשניות, סנהדרין. ברוב ההוצאות של התלמוד בבלי, מסכת סנהדרין (בסוף המסכתא).

———. פירוש המשניות, הוצאת "ראשונים": אוצר הקדמות. תל-אביב, תש"ח/1948 (הדפסות אחרות ע"י מוסד הרב קוק, בירושלים).

———. משנה תורה, קושטא, רס"ט/1509 (צלום: ירושלים, תשכ"ה).

———. משנה תורה. עם השגות הראב"ד. ברוב ההוצאות של הרמב"ם משנת רס"ט והלאה.

———. מורה נבוכים. תרגום ר'שמואל אבן תבון. ווארשא, תרל"ב/1872 (הדפסות אחרות, בווילנא ובווארשא וצלומים מזה בני-יורק, תש"ז).

———. קובץ תשובות הרמב"ם ואגרותיו.לפסיא, תרי"ט/1859 (צלום מזה: ירושלים, תשכ"ז; פארנבורו, 1969).

———. תשובות הרמב"ם, הוצאת א.ח. פריימן, ירושלים: "מקיצי נרדמים", תרצ"ד/1934.

———. תשובות הרמב"ם, הוצאת יהושע בלאו. 3 כרכים. ירושלים: "מקיצי נרדמים", תשי"ח-תשכ"ג.

———. אגרות הרמב"ם, בעריכת מ.ד. רבינוביץ. תל-אביב: הוצאת "ראשונים", (הדפסות אחרות: ירושלים: מוסד הרב קוק).

———. אגרות הרמב"ם, בעריכת ד"צ בענט, ירושלים: הוצאת "מקיצי נרדמים", תש"ו/1946.

ר' משה בן נחמן: כל כתבי הרמב"ן, בעריכת ח. שבל. ירושלים: מוסד הרב קוק, תשכ"ד/1964.

משניות. ששה סדרי משנה, מפורשים בידי ח. אלבק. סדר נזיקין, ירושלים: מוסד ביאליק, תשי"ז/1957.

המשנה אשר עליה נוסד התלמוד הירושלמי, הוצאת ו.ה. לו. קמבריג', 1883 (דפוס צלום: ירושלים, תשכ"ז).

סדר אליהו רבא, הוצאת ר"מ איש שלום (פרידמן), וינה, תרמ"ב/1882.

סדר עבודת ישראל, בעריכת ר"י בער. רעדעלהיים. תרכ"ח/1868.

ר' סעדיה גאון: אמונות ודעות. ברלין, 1928.

עזריה מן האדומים: מאור עינים, בעריכת י"ט צונץ. וילנה, 1863.

פוגלמן, ר' מרדכי: בית מרדכי שאלות ותשובות. ירושלים: מוסד הרב קוק, תשל"א/1970.

קאפח, ר' יוסף: קצת לדרך התרגום. **הצופה**, כ"ט כסלו, תשכ"ט.

קסובסקי, ח"י.: אוצר לשון התלמוד, כרך 1‏ 39. ירושלים, תשט"ז‏/1956—תשל"ח‏/1978 (הולך ונדפס).

——. אוצר לשון המשנה. 4 כרכים. ירושלים, 1956‏-1960.

——. אוצר לשון התוספתא. ירושלים, 1932‏-1961.

רבינוביץ, ר"נ: דקדוקי סופרים, סנהדרין. מינכן, תרל"ח‏/1878.

שטיינשניידר, משה: ציונים לתולדות ר' זרחיה הלוי בן יצחק בן שאלתיאל חן. **אוצר נחמד**, 2 (תרי"ז‏/1857), 229‏-245.

שם טוב בן שם טוב. ספר האמונות, פירארא, שיו שי"‏ז/1556.

תא‑שמע, י.: יצירתו הספרותית של ר' מאיר הלוי אבולעאפיא. **קרית ספר**, 43 (1968), 569‏-576.

Manuscripts

1. Cambridge. MS. R.8.26(2). *Perush Ḥeleq, le-ha-RaMbaM.* (E. H. Palmer, *A Descriptive Catalogue of the Arabic . . . Manuscripts in the Library of Trinity College . . . with an Appendix . . . of the Hebrew . . . MSS . . . A 23370.* pp. 244–45. Cambridge-London, 1870).

2. Cambridge. Genizah. T-S. K 27, no. 6 published by L. N. Goldfeld in Kobez al-Yad, vol. 10, 1982.

3. Cambridge. Add. 507. 1. *ʾIggeret sheluḥa meʾet ha-rav Asher . . . ʿal ʾodot Moreh ha-Nevukhim lērabanei Zarefat.*

4. Oxford. The Bodleian. No. 2493³ (Neubauer Catalogue of Hebrew MSS). *ʾIggeret sheshalaḥ ha-RaMbaM al Teḥiyyat ha-Metim.*

5. Oxford. The Bodleian. (No. 577 Neubauer Catalogue of Hebrew MSS). MS. Huntingdon 80. The Jewish National and University Library, microfilm no. 19448.—Moses ben Maimon-*Mishneh Torah.*

Appendix
The Hebrew Text of Yad Ramah

יד רמה
מסכת סנהדרין
פרק חלק

דפוס שלוניקי תקנ"ח

1. ד"ץ כל ישראל יש להם חלק לעה"ב כו' הכי אשכחן בנוסחי עתיקי ודייקי דסמכי פרק חלק לאלו הן הנשרפין בין בנסחי דמתני' בין בנסחי דגמ' והכי נמי מסתברא מדאתחיל לפרושי נהרגין באלו הן הנשרפין דקתני ואלו הן הנהרגין הרוצח ואנשי עיר הנדחת אי אמרת בשלמא פרק חלק בתר אלו הן הנשרפין הוי היני דסליק ממילי דרוצח וקא מפרש מילי דאנשי עיר הנדחת לאסוקי נהרגין מיניהו בפ' אלו הנשרפין. אלא אי אמרת דאלו הנחנקין תנן מקמי פרק חלק אכתי לא פריש מילי דנהרגין וקא נקיט לפרושי נחנקין אלא ודאי ש"מ דפרק חלק תנן ברישא ואיידי דאיירי בסוף אלו הן הנשרפין בזר שטימ' דהוי בידי שמי' נקט לפרושי הני דמסי[ק] היניהו בידי שמי' לעה"ב והיינו דקתני דכל ישראל יש להן חלק לעה"ב.

2. וענין העה"ב יסוד גדול מיסודי התורה הוא שהרי הכופר בו אעפ"י שיש בידו תורה ומעשים טובים אין לו חלק לעה"ב כדמפרש במתני' ומוסיף לה בירורא בגמ' ולא עוד אלא שצדוק דינו של הקב"ה תלוי בו לומר שעיניו פקוחות על כל דרכי בני אדם לתת לאיש כדרכיו וכפרי מעלליו לפיכך צריכין אנו לפרש ענינו לפי מה שקבלנו מאבותינו ומרבותינו ולפי הקבלה הפשוטה ביד כל ישראל גם לפי פשטן של משניות והשמועות לא להתעולל עלילות ולבקש גדולות ולהרהר אחר קבלת אבותינו ולחדש דבר בדעתינו הקלה והמעוטא ולחקור אחר הנסתרות אשר הם לה' אלהינו ואין לנו עסק בהן לדעת מה זה ועל מה זה.

3. וענין העה"ב הוא הזמן ההוה אחר ימות המשיח בכמה שנים ועיקר מתן שכרן של צדיקים ועונשין לרשעים אינו בו כדתנן באבות העה"ז דומה לפרוזדור בפני העה"ב התקן עצמך בפרוזדור כדי שתכנס לטרקלין וכן עונשן של רשעים אינו אלא לעה"ב כדדרשינן בפרקין הכרת תכרת בעה"ז תכרת לעה"ב.

4. ואעפ"י שהשכר והעונש שניהן בעה"ב הן יש מקומות שאין לשון לעה"ב נופל אלא על מתן שכרן בלבד ולא על העונש כגון הא דתנן בפרקין כל ישראל יש להן חלק לעה"ב וכן ההיא דתנן התם העה"ז דומה לפרוזדור בפני העה"ב דמשמע שאם לא התקנת עצמך בפרוזדור אי אתה נכנס לעה"ב ואין דברים הללו אמורין אלא על השכר שבו ולא על העונש וכן הא דתנן בפרקין לקמן אנשי סדום אין להם חלק לעה"ב לא אמרו אלא על השכר שבו ולא על העונש מדקתני אבל עומדין בדין. ואין צריך לומר בכל מקום שנאמ' חיי העה"ב שעל השכר בלבד נאמר.

5. והעה"ב האמור במשנתינו לפי פשטן של משניות ודברי התלמוד וגם לפי הקבלה הפשוטה בכל ישראל הוא עמידת הגויות והנפשות לדין כאחת כאשר היו קודם מיתתן שהרי כתבנו שאין שכרן של צדיקים ועונשן של רשעים אלא לעה"ב

לפי' אי אפשר בלא גוף כדמוכח מדאמר ליה אנטונינוס לרבי יכולין גוף ונשמה
לפטור את עצמן מן הדין כדמפרש בגמ' לקמן וראיה נמי ליום הדין שאי אפשר אלא
בתחיית המתים דתנן הוא היה אומר הילודים למות והמתי' להחיות והחיים לידון
הא למדת שאחרי הולדתם הם מתים ואחר מיתתן הן חיים ואחר חייהן הם נידונין ומתני'
וגמ' דילה נמי דייקי דקתני ואלו שאין להן חלק לעה"ב האומר אין תחיית המתים
ואמרי' בגמ' וכל כך למה ומהדרינן לפי שכל מדותיו של הקב"ה מדה כנגד מדה הוא
כפר בתחיית המתים לפיכך לא יהא חלק בתחיית המתים הא למדת שהעה"ב השנוי
במשנתינו זהו תחיית המתים. ועוד מדדרשי' לקמן מניין לתחיית המתים כו' שנאמר
הכרת תכרת הכרת בעה"ז תכרת לעה"ב ואמר ריב"ל מניין לתחיית המתים מן התורה
שנאמר עוד יהללוך סלה הללוך לא נאמר אלא יהללוך מכאן לתחיית המתים וקי"ל
דלעולם הבא קאמר דאמר ריב"ל גופיה כל האומר שירה בעה"ז זוכה ואומרה לעה"ב
שני' יהללוך סלה הללוך לא נאמר אלא יהללוך הא למדת שהעה"ב יש בו תחיית
המתים.

6.   ועוד דגרסי' בברכות מרגלא בפומיה דרב העוה"ב אין בו לא אכילה ולא
שתיה ולא משא ולא מתן לא פריה ולא רביה אלא צדיקים יושבים ועטרות' בראשיהן
ונהנין מזיו השכינה ואם אין הגויות חיות לעה"ב מפני מה הוצרכו לומר שאין בו
כל אלו היה להן לומר שאין בו גוף ונמצאו כל אלו בטלין מאליהן, אלא לומר לך
שאעפ"י שיש בו גויות אין בו אכילה ושתייה ולפי' הוצרך לומר אלא צדיקים
יושבין ועטרותיהן בראשיהן ונהנין מזיו שכינה כלום' וכי מאחר שאין בו כל אלו
צדיקים ממה הן נהנין ומה יהא על שכרן והשיב יושבין ועטרותיהן בראשיהן
ונהנין מזיו שכינה.

7.   וקראי נמי מוכחין דיום דינא לא סגייא אלא בתחיית המתים דכתיב ורבים
מישיני אדמת עפר יקיצו אלה לחיי עולם ואלה לחרפות לדראון עולם וכתיב יקרא
אל השמים מעל ואל הארץ לדין עמו וכדאמר ליה רבי לאנטונינוס והרי בארנו
מפשוטן של פסוקים וכח המשניגי' והשמועות שהעה"ב שמשלמין בו שכר לצדיקים
ונפרעין בו מן הרשעים אי אפשר בלא גוף וכן קבלה פשוטה ביד כל ישראל איש
מפי איש הלכה למשה מסיני וכ"כ רבינו סעדיה ז"ל בספר האמונות וכן כתבו כל
הגאונים בספרי'.

8.   וכן הדעת נוטה לכך שכשם שמדת הדין נותנת לשלם שכר לנפש על ישרה
וליפרע הימנה על מעלה כך מדת הדין נותנת לשלם שכר לגויה על ישרה וליפרע
על מעלה שהרי שניהם עשו מעשה אם טוב ואם רע ואם אין הגויות חיות איה איפה
תקותה ותקותם מי ישורנה ומי ישיב גמול לגוף על ישרו ועל מעלו והוא עשה
מי ישלם לו.

9.   וא"ת שאין הגוף נידון שאלמלא נשמה הרי הוא כאבן שאין לה הופכין גם

הנשמה לא תידון שאלמלא הגוף אין חטא בא על ידה וכדאמר ליה אנטונינוס לרבי
יכולין גוף ונשמה לפטור את עצמן מן הדין.

10. ואם יש שמדקדקין ואומרין והלא הגוף לנשמה ככלי מעשה לאדם ואם נאמר
שהגוף נדון לפי שנעשה מעשה על ידו א"כ גם חרבו וקשתו וכל כליו שנעשה מעשה
על ידן ידונו שתי תשובות בדבר הראשונה שאין מעשה גופו של אדם דומה למעשה
חרבו וקשתו ושאר כליו משני פנים הפנים הראשונים שאעפ"י שאין הגוף עושה
מעשה אלא לפי מחשבת הנפש ועצתה אינו עושה מכח הנפש בלבד שא"כ
היה בדין שלא כח הגוף ולא יחזק אלא לפי כח הנפש אבל הכלי העושה מעשה
מכח אדם המניפו בלבד אינו עושה מעשה אלא לפי כח המניף אם מעט הרבה
ולפי מחשבתו אם טובה ואם רעה והנך רואה בעיניך שאין כח הגוף תלוי בכח
הנפש, שפעמים רבות שיקרה מקרה לגוף בלבד וימעט כחו אעפ"י שלא נגרע מכח
הנפש דבר ונמצא שאין הגוף עושה מעשה מכח הנפש בעל כרחו כאשר הכלי עושה
מעשה בעל כרחו לפי' דין הוא שידון הגוף ולא ידון הכלי והפנים השנים שמדת
הדין נותנת שיהא גופו של אדם נידון ולא יהא הכלי נידון ולא מקבל שכר לפי שגופו
של אדם יש בו רוח חיים ונמצא מרגיש בכל מה שהוא עושה ויש בו דעת לעשות
טוב ורע אבל הכלי אין בו אחת מכל אלו. והתשובה השנית לפי שגופו של אדם
כשהוא נידון אינו נידון לבדו אלא עם הנפש כאשר היה זה בשעת מעשה וכן מדת
הדין נותנת כאהדר ליה רבי לאנטונינוס לפיכך דין הוא שידון שהרי הוא מרגיש
בעונשו ובשכרו ונמצא שאין דינו יוצא לבטלה אבל הכלי אפי' העמידוהו כמו שהיה
בשעה שנעשה מעשה על ידו דינו יוצא לבטלה ואין הקב"ה עושה דבר לבטלה
ואין נכון לומר שיתן כח בכלי כדי שירגיש בעונשו ובשכרו שא"כ לקתה מדת הדין
כיצד זה עושה שלא מדעת ולוקה מדעת.

11. ויש מגדולי הדור שמודים בתחיית המתים שתהיה בימות המשיח ואומרי'
שמתים שחיין בימות המשיח ארוכים מאד בחיים הארוכים ההם שעתידי'
להיות בימות המשיח ואח"כ מתים אבל חיי העה"ב אחר ימות המשיח שמשלמין
בו שכר לצדיקים ואין בו מות ונפרעין בו מן הרשעים אין בו גוף ולא גויה אלא
נפשות הצדיקים בלא גוף כמלאכי השרת ומביאין ראיה לדבריהם מאשר אמרו חכמים
העה"ב אין בו לא אכילה ולא שתייה לומר שכיון שאין בו אכילה ושתיה אין בו גוף
ולא גויה וזהו דעת הרמב"ם ז"ל בהל' תשובה בפ"ח.

12. והיינו סבורין מתחילה כי היה טעמו לפי שאי אפשר לגוף שיהיה לעולם
בלא אכילה ושתיה לפי' השבנו על דבריו באגרתנו השלוחה ללוניל. וזה נוסח דברינו
שם בענין זה ואם יש אומרי' איך יעמיד גויה בלי אכילה ושתיה עצת רשעים רחקה
מני. הממציא הגוף מאין טרם היותו לאין יכו' להעמידו מבלי אכל ושתה הלא ציר
נאמן עמד בהר סיני מ' יום ומ' לילה לחם לא אכל ומים לא שתה גם אליהו כה עשה
עד בואו הר השם חורב גם מים הלקחו עד היום הזה.

13. וכי יאמר חיה יחיו אך ימותו אחרי עומדם אל תבוא נפשי בסודם כי האמנם
אם לכוד ילכדוני עוד חבלי שאול במוקשם למה לי חיים טוב לי עוד אני שם והנה
השם צבאות יעץ ומי יפר וידו הנטויה ומי ישיבנה ההוא אמר ולא יעשה ודבר
ולא יקימנה לאמר בלע המות לנצח ואומר ומצדיקי הרבים ככוכבים לעולם ועד
וכי יאמר כי און ילין בקרבה ח"ו מהצדיק כל מדבר בה. הממציא הגויות טרם
היותם הלא יוכל להעמידם אחרי חיותם בנפשותם וגויותם עד הנה דברי תשובתי
בענין הזה באגרתי הראשונה השלוח' ללוניל' ועוד נוסף עליהם באגרתי האחרונה
דברים רבים כאלה.

14. וכהנה וכהנה השי' על דבריו רב שמואל גאון הממונה ראש ישיבה בבבל בדורנו
זה וכן שאלונו על זאת מאספאהאן ומארץ תימן כי הבינו כולם לפי מחשבתם מתוך
דבריו שלא היה מודה בתחיית המתים כלל ושם נקרא אנשי בליעל תלמידים שהיו
כופרים בתחיית המתים וכשהתריסו אנשי מקומם כנגדן הביאו להם ראיה מדברי הרב
האמורים בה' תשובה והוצרכו אנשי המקום לשלוח לרב על זאת לעמוד על דעתו
בדבר הזה והשיב להם תשובה על זאת והאריך בענין הזה הרבה והוסי' בה ענינים
אחרים שאינן מענין דברינו זה והנגנו כותבים עניני תשובתו בדבר הזה בדרך קצרה.

15. תחילת ענין התשובה היתה לנקות את עצמו מהשם ומישראל על דבר כל
אמונת תחיית המתי' אשר חשדוהו החושדים עליה והעתיק המעתיק את דבריו בלשון
ערבי ללשון הקדש בלשון קשה עד מאד אך הנני כותב מקצת לשונו הפשוט בעיני
ואשנה מקצתו לבאר עניני הדברים אשר נתכון המחבר לאומרם כאשר תשיג ידי.

16. ואלה עניני דבריו בדבר הזה בדרך קצרה דע אתה המעיין שכונתנו במאמר
הזה הוא לבאר מה שנאמין בו בפנה הזאת אשר נפלו הדברים בין התלמידים והיא
תחיית המתים המפורסמת באומתינו אשר רב זכרה בתפילות ובסיפורים ובתחילות
אשר חברום הנביאים וגדולי החכמים שמלאו מהם דברי התלמוד והמדרשות ענינה
שוב הנפש הזאת לגוף אחרי הפרדה ממנו ודבר זה הוא דבר שלא נשמע באומה
מחלוקת עליו ואין בו פתרון זולתי פשטו כלל ואסור להאמין באיש מאנשי הדת
שהוא מאמין בחילוף דבר זה בתחיית המתים זו היא תשו' הנפש והגו' אח' המות
כבר זכר' דניאל זכרון שאי אפש' לפותרו פתרון אחר באומרו ורבים מישיני אדמת עפר
יקיצו אלה לחיי עולם ואלה לחרפות לדראון עולם. ואמר לו המלאך ואתה לך לקץ
ותנוח ותעמוד לגורלך לקץ הימין ועוד כתב ב"ר וכן יראה לנו שאנשים האלה אשר
תשובנה נפשו' לגופות ההם יאכלו וישתו וישמשו מטותיהם ויולידו וימותו אחר
חיים ארוכים מאד כחיים הנמצאים בימות המשיח.

17. ואמנם החיים שאין מות אחריה' הם חיי העה"ב כיון שאין בהם גוף לפי שאנחנו
נאמין בדבר שהוא אמת בעיני כל בן דעת שהעה"ב נפשות מבלתי גופות כמלאכים
וביאור הדבר הזה שהגו' אמנם הוא כלל כלים לפעולות הנפש וכבר התבאר זה

הדבר במופת וכל מה שבגו' יחלק לג' חלקים כלים שיגמר בהם המזון בפה ובאסטומכא
והיא הנקרא בלשון ערבי מעדה והכבד ובני מעים ובכללם כל מה שבתוך הבטן
התחתון וכלים שתהיה בהם ההולדה והם כלי התשמיש והולדת הזרע והולדת העובר
וכלים שבהם יהיה תיקון עניני הגו' עד שימציא לעצמו כל מה שיצטרך אליו כעינים
ושאר החושים ומיני הגידים החלולים ושאינם חלולין כגון גידים הנקראין בלשון
ערבי עצב והמיתרים אשר בהם ישלמו התנועות כולם ולולי אלו לא היה אפשר
לבעל חיים להתנועע אל מזונו ולברוח ממה שכנגדו שמאבדו ומפסיד מזגו וכאשר
לא ישלם הממון רק במלאכות שיעשם ובהזמנ' רבות שיצטרך בהם לחשב ולהשתכל
נמצא לו הכח השכלי לזכור בו המלאכות ההם ונמצא לו כן כלים טבעיים לעשות
בהם המלאכות ההם רצוני לומר הידים והרגלים כי הרגלים אינם כלי להליכה בלבד
ופרטי זה הכלל נודעים אצל אנשי החכמ' הנה כבר התבא' שהגו' כולו צריך המצאו
מבלי תכלי' א' והיא קבלת המז' להתמד' הגו' והולדת הדומה לו להתיחדות מין הגו'
ההוא וכשתהיה התכלית ההיא מסולקת מבלי היות צריך אליה רצוני לומר בעה"ב
שכבר ביארו לנו המון החכמים שאין בו לא אכי' ולא שתי' א"כ הוא ביאור להעדר
הגו' שהקב"ה יתעלה לא ימציא דבר לבטלה כלל ולא יעשה דבר אלא מפני דבר
וחלילה לו וחס שיהיו פעולותיו המתוקנות כפעולות עובדי הצלמים אשר עינים להם
ולא יראו אזנים להם ולא ישמעו אף להן ולא יריחון כן הקב"ה אצל אלו יברא גופות
כלומר איברים שלא לעשות בהם מה שנבראו בעבורו כלל ולא לשום סיבה ואולי
בני העה"ב אצל אלו אלו אנשים אינם בעלי איברים אך הם גופות על כל פנים ואולי הם
עגולים ככידור או ארוכים כצורת העמודים או מרובעין בארכן וברחבן ובקומתם
וריבועו שוה לכל רוח כצורת העקב ואין אלו אלו אלא שחוק ומי יתן והחרש החרישון
ותהי להם לחכמה והסיבה בכל זאת מה שביארנוהו מהיות ההמון אין בעיניהם מציאות
אלא לגוף או מה שימצא בגוף ומה שאינו גוף ולא בגו' אינו נמצא בעיניהם וכל
אשר ירצו לחזק המציא[ות] ענין אחד יוסיפוהו גויות רצוני לומר יוסיפו עבה לעצם
גויתו עד הנה דבריו בענין הזה בדרך קצרה.

18. ועוד כתב בתשובה ההיא וכבר נסתפקו ג"כ אנשים אחרים כדברינו בסוף
החיבור במקום שאמרנו דבר שזה לשונו אל יעלה על דעתך שהמלך המשיח צריך
לעשות אותות ומופתים ומחדש דברים בעולם או מחיה מתים וכיוצא בדברים אלו
כו' והבאנו ראיה על זה כמה שבארנוהו וחשבו קצת חלושי העיון זאת ההכחשה
לתחיית המתים ואנחנו לא אמרנו זולתי שהמשיח לא יבקש ממנו שיעשה מופת
שיבקע ים או יחיה מת על דרך המופת מפני שאין מופת מבוקש ממנו אחרי שיעדונו
בו הנביאים אשר נאמרה נבואתם ולא יתחיי' מהמאמר הזה לומר שהשם לא יחיה
המתים ברצונו כשירצה ולמי שירצה אם בימי המשיח או לפניו או אחרי מותו עד
כה דבריו בענין הזה ועוד נוסף עליהם דברים רבים שאינו עתידים להביאם בפרק זה
בעזרת ה' אלא שאינם מענין דברינו זה שהתחלנו לדבר בענין העה"ב.

19. ואחרי אשר סדרו דבריו בענין העה"ב שאין בו גוף לפי סברתו נתחיל לכתוב

סברנו וטעמנו בעה"ב שאין בו אכילה ושתיה לומר שיש בו גוף וגויה כאשר כתבו
חכמי המחקר מן הגאונים הראשונים וגם לפי הקבלה הפשוטה ביד כל ישראל וגם
השמועה אשר הביא ראיה ממנה היה לנו לעדה כי העה"ב שאמרו שאין בו אכילה
ושתיה יש בו גוף וגויה שאם אין בו גוף וגויה מפני מה הוצרך לומר שאין בו כל
אלו היה לו לומר שאין בו גוף ונמצאו כל אלו בטלין מאיליהן וכי אלו אמר שאין
בו גוף כלום תעלה על דעת אדם שיש בו אכילה ושתיה או משא ומתן ופריה ורביה
וכבר בארנו דבר זה פעם אחרת בתחילת דברנו זה.

20. ועוד לדבריו הרי הנפש יכולה לפטור את עצמה מן הדין כשאלת אנטונינוס לר'.
ואע"ת שאין הגויות מקבלות עונשן ולא שכרן אלא בימות המשיח מה יהא עליהן
לעה"ב ומה יתרון נפש הצדיק על גופו לעה"ב שהנפש זוכה לחיים שאין להם הפסק
והגוף אינו זוכה לכך אם בעבור מעלת הנפש בעצמה שהיא טהורה וזכה מן הגו'
הלא אב אחד לכולם אל אחד בראם וכי והלא יד שניהם שוה בין בצדקת' בין
ברשעתם במה זכתה הנפש יתר מן הגו' עוד שהרי משנה שלימה שנינו באנשי סדום
שאין להם חלק לעה"ב אבל עומדין בדין ומראין הדברים שעמידה זו בדין לעה"ב
היא ממ"ש בעדת צדיקים אינן עומדין אבל עומדין הן בעדת רשעים ונראין הדברים
שאין להם חלק בשכר אבל עומדין בדין לקבל עונשן.

21. ואם תאמר שהעולם הבא אין בו לא גוף ולא גויה נמצאת אומר שעמידת
הרשעים בדין לעה"ב בנפשות לבדן הם וא"כ מה יתרון לגוף הרשע על נפשו שנפשו
עומדת בדין לקבל ענשה וגופו אינו עומד בדין לקבל עונשו ועוד א"כ נמצא לגוף
הרשע יתרון על נפשו ולנפש הצדיק יתרון על גופו.

22. ואם תאמר שנפש הרשע נכרתת בהכרת גויתו בימות המשיח או בסופן א"כ
מי ברשעים עומד בדין לעולם הבא אם גופן הרי כבר מת ואם נפשם הרי כבר
נכרתה והשם לנפש מעלה יתירה בדין על הגו' נראה מדעתו שאין השכר והעונש
לעולם הבא לפי מעשיה' של בריות ולפי מדת הדין אלא לפי הטבע שהנפש שיש
בטבעה להשאר תשאר והגו' שטבעו לכלות יכלה ונמצאת מדת הדין לוקה בשני
העולמות בעולם הזה ובעולם הבא וגם נפש הצדיק והרשע לפי הרעה הזאת אינן
נידונות לפי מעשיהם אלא לפי דעתן לפי שהנפש שיודעת את בוראה במופתי החכמה
היא נשארת מפני מדת הדעת שבה שהיא קיימת לעולם והנפש שאינה יודעת את בוראה
במופתי החכמה תכרת אעפ"י שיש בידה תורה ומעשים טובים ונמצא שאין לתורה
ולמעשים טובים יתרון לעולם הואיל והדבר תלוי בטבע שאם תאמר יש להן יתרון
נמצא שאין הדבר תלוי בטבע אלא כל אחד ואחד ניד[ו]ן לפי מעשיו גם לפי אהבתו
ויראתו ודעותיו ונמצא דין הגו' ודין הנפש שוין לעולם הבא הואיל ושניהם שוין
במעשיה' אם טובים ואם רעים.

23. ואם מפני הטעם שאמר הרב באגרתו כי מאחר שהעולם הבא אין בו לא אכילה

ולא שתייה ולא תשמיש נמצאו איברי הגו' העשויין לכל אלו בלבד ונראין לבטלה
אין הקב"ה עושה דבר לבטלה, כשאתה מדקדק בדבר אתה מוצא שאין תחיית הגופות
לעולם הבא לבטלה מפני שלשה טעמים. הטעם הראשון לפי שמדת הדין נותנת
שיקבלו הגופות ענשן או שכרן בנפשות הואיל ושניהם שוין במעשה אם טוב ואם
רע. ואם תאמר אם כן ישמשו האיברים מעין מלאכתן ואל תהי בריאת האיברים ההם
לבטלה אינם לבטלה שהרי יש בהם מעלת מעלה גדולה להודיע לבאי עולם גבורתו של
מקום שהוא יכול להחיות את הגויות לעולם בלי אכילה ושתייה ושהוא יכול לברוא
איברים שיש בטבען להתאוות לאכילה ושתייה ולפריה ורביה ולתשמיש והוא יכול
לשנות את טבעם כדי שלא יתאוו לדברים ההם אעפ"י שלא חסר בהם ולא אודע.

24. ומצאנו דוגמת דבר זה באכיל' המן ויענך וירעיבך כו' למען הודיעך כי לא על
הלחם לבדו יחיה האדם כי ע"כ מוצא פי ה' יחיה האדם. ועוד שמדת הדין נותנת
שיקבל כל אבר ואבר ענשו או שכרו בדרך שהיה בשעת רשעתו או צדקתו וכיון
שמדת הדין של קב"ה נותנת להשפיע לצדיקים כזאת שיחיו בלי אכילה ושתיה ובלי
עמל וצער ונהנין מזיו שכינה שהיא מעלה גדולה עד מאד ואין לנבראות מעלה
גדולה ממנה הרי הגו' והנפש שוין בה שכיון שמדת הגופות והנפשות שוה בדין
שיזכו שניהם למעלה זו.

25. והתמה הגדול בעיני חוץ מכל זה לדברי הרב שנתן טעם לדבריו בהעדר הגו'
לפי שאין הקב"ה עושה דבר לבטלה ואם יוכ' לומר כן על מה יעשה בגויות הרשעים
והלא הדין נותן שיברא להם איברים שיש בהן תאוה כדי שתתמנע מהן תאותם כענין
שנאמר וימנע מרשעים אורם ואין דבר זה לבטלה ועוד תמה אני אם יוכל להעמיד
את הברייתא השנויה בשם תנא דבי אליהו שעתיד הקב"ה להחיות בימו'
המשיח שוב אינן חוזרין לעפרן אלא אם הוציא' כי מפשטה לומר שמתים הללו האמורים
בה לא מתים ממש הם אלא העולים מבור הגלות הם הנקראים כאן מתים שעתיד
הקב"ה להחיותן לימות המשיח ומהו שאמרו אינם חוזרים לעפרן שאינם חוזרים
לגלות ולעניות שהיו בו מתחלה כענין שנאמר בתמורת הענין הזה מקים מעפר
דל אלא שאין אנו יודעים איך יוכל לפתור מה שאמרו.

26. ואם תאמר אותם אלף שנים שהקב"ה מחדש את עולמו צדיקים מה תהא
עליהם כו' ועוד אם לא דברה הברייתא אלא בעולים מבור הגלות שאינם חוזרים
לגלותם למה דברה בלשון סתום וכי להטעות את הבריות באה. ואי אתה יכול
לדמו' דבר זה לשאר דברים הכתובים והאמורים דרך משל לפי שאי אתה מוצא
בדבר האמור על דרך כזו אלא מפני אחד משני טעמים. הראשון בזמן שאין הלשון
יכולה לבאר את הענין לבריו' אלא ע"י משל ודמיון כעין לשון איברים האמורים
במקום יתעלה מכל זה וכו' וכיוצא בה אמרו חכמים דברה תורה כלשון בני אדם.
והטעם השני בזמן שהענין ההוא ראוי לסתמו מן הבריות כענין הקץ שנאמר לדניאל
בלשון סתום וזרוזהו לסתום את הדברי' מפני שהיה רחוק מאד מן העת ההיא שנ'

בה ואלו נודע בעת ההיא שהיה רחוק כל כך כמה מרשעי ישראל היו אז וגם עתה שהיו יוצאים מן הכלל אבל בריתא זו אין בה אחת מכל אלו.

27. ואלו לא דברה אלא בעולין מעפר דלותן וגלותן לומר שאין חוזרין לאותו עפר למה סתמה את דבריה וכי להטע׳ את הבריות היא צריכה להבטיחן בדבר שאינו עתיד להיו׳ ואע״פ שאי אפשר לומר שאין בריתא זו שנויה אלא לדברי האומר במתים שהחיה יחזקאל באמת משל היה אבל לדברי האומר שהיו ואחר כך מתו ילפינן ממתים שהחיה יחזקאל כדאמרי׳ עלה בהדיא וניל׳ ממתים שמתו לאח׳ עמידתן והשבנו סבר לה כמאן דאמר באמת משל היה.

28. ועוד יש ללמוד משם שאין דברי הברית׳ הזאת דברי קבלה אלא דברי סברא בעלמא שאלו היו דברי קבלה היאך היה עולה על דעתנו ללמוד ממתים שהחיה יחזקאל וכי מפני שמתו אלו נכפור בקבלה שבידינו במתים שעתידין להיו׳ בימו׳ המשיח ונתחייב לומר שכל המתים שעתידין להיו׳ סופן למות ומאחר שאמרו שיש ללמוד מן המתים שהחיה יחזקאל נראה שדברי התנא מסברא הם שיש רשות לחולק לחלוק על בריתא זו ולו׳ שמתים שעתיד הקב״ה להחיותן לימי׳ המשיח חוזרין לעפרן אפ״ה דוקא בימי׳ המשיח אבל לעוה״ב הכל מודים שם אין מיתה דנאמר בלע המות לנצח ולא מפני שאין בו גוף שהרי שהרי המשניו׳ והשמועו׳ שאין בהם מחלוק׳ מעידו׳ שיש גוף כאשר ביארנו.

29. ואם תשאל לדברינו שאמרנו שהעוה״ב השנוי במשנתנו הוא העוה״ב באחרונה אחרי ימי׳ המשיח והוא העולם שמשלמין בו שכר לצדיקים ונפרעים בו מן הרשעים וכבר נתברר לדברי הכל שאין בו לא אכילה ולא שתיה א״כ מה ראיה להם מן הפסוק שנאמר בו לעולם יירשו ארץ וכי מאחר שאין אכילה ושתיה ירושה זו למה וארץ זו למה וכי יש שם קנאה או מלחמה או חסרון כל דבר כדי שיביטיחם בירושת הארץ כדי שיאכלו פירותיה ויקחו להם כספה וזהבה ומראין הדברים שאין משנה זו מדברת אלא בימי׳ המשיח שיש בו אכי׳ ושתיה והוא הנקרא כאן העולם הבא וכן תחיית המתים האמור בההיא כההיא תחיית המתים העתידה להיות בימות המשיח.

30. ועוד ראיה לדבר מדרבי יוחנן דא״ר יוחנן מנין לתחיית המתים מן התורה שנאמר ונתתה ממנו תרומת ה׳ לאהרן הכהן וכי אהרן לעולם קיים שנותנין לו תרומה אלא מלמד שעתיד לחיו׳ וישר׳ נותנין לו מתנו׳ מכאן לתה״מ מן התורה ותה״ה זו אין להעמידה אלא בימו׳ המשיח אבל לעוה״ב דא״כ מתנו׳ הללו מה טיבן והלא אין בו אכילה ושתיה וכן כל הני קראי דמיתו רבנן בגמרא מינייהו ראיה לתח״ה כגון למען ירבו ימיכם כו׳ וכי הא דכתיב אז יבנה יהושע מזבח וכגון הא דכתיב קול צופיך נשאו ק״י ירננו כולהו הני ומאי דדמי להו בימות המשיח קא מיירו וכן הא דכתיב ורבים מישיני אדמת עפר יקיצו אלה לחיי עולם ואלה לחרפות לדראון עולם מראין הדברים שעל מתים שחיין בימות המשיח נאמר שהרי דבר הלמד מעניינו

וזה שנאמר אלה לחיי עולם לומר לך שצדיקים שעתיד הקב״ה להחיות בימות המשיח
שוב אינם חוזרים לעפרן כדמוכח בגמ׳ לקמן מקרא אחרינא וזה שנאמר ואלה לחרפות
לדראון עולם לומר לך שיש מן המתים שחיין בימות המשיח שחיין לקבל עונשן שאין
עונשן של רשעים מתחיל מן העוה״ב בלבד אלא שאף בימות המשיח יש רשעים
גמורים שהם עומדים לקב׳ עונשן מן העת ההיא והלא לדורי דורות ועליהם נאמר
ואלה לחרפות לדראון עולם.

31. ונמצאנו בנביאים שאמרו כיוצא בזו בישעיה הוא אומר ויצאו וראו כו׳ ובימות
המשיח הכתו׳ מדבר שהרי דבר הלמד מעניינו דכתיב מקמי הכי והביאו את כל
אחיכם מכל הגוים מנחה לה׳ וכן במלאכי הוא או׳ הנני שולח מלאכי כו׳ ופנה דרך לפני
כו׳ ובימות המשיח קאי כדמוכח מדכתיב ופתאם יבוא אל היכלו האדון אשר אתם
מבקשים וזהו המלך המשיח וכתיב וקרבתי אלכם למשפט והייתי עד ממהר במכשפים
ובמנאפים הרי ענשן של רשעים אמור וזה שנאמר ומצדיקי הרבים ככוכבי לעולם
ועד דמשמע שהם עומדים ככוכבים שעומדין לעולם ועד כמצדיקי הרבים שחיין
בימות המשיח נאמר אע״פ שכבר נאמר עליהן אלה לחיי עולם שלא תאמר עולם
זה יש לו קצבה כענין שנאמר ועבדו לעולם לפיכך הוצרך להוסי׳ פירוש לדבר לו׳
לעולם ועד לומר שאין לזמן זה קצבה כענין שנאמר ה׳ ימלוך לעולם ועד לו שאין לו
קצבה.

32. וצריכין אנו עוד לפרש לך שזה שנאמר כאן לעולם ועד לא על מצדיקי הרבים
בלבד נאמר אלא גם על המשכילים נאמר וכן פירוש הדברים והמשכילים יזהירו כזוהר
הרקיע ומצדיקי הרבים יזהירו ככוכבים וכולם עומדים לעולם ועד וכן הא דכתיב
ואתה לך לקץ ותנוח ותעמוד לגורלך לקץ הימין שהוא פסוק מוכיח על תחיית
המתים שהרי יעדו בשלשה זמנים הראשון בעודו חי בעוה״ז וזהו שנאמר לו לך
לקץ כלומר ואתה לך עתה עד שיגיע הקץ כענין שנאמר לו קודם לכן לך לך דניאל
כי סתומי׳ וחתומי׳ כו׳ והזמן השני לעת פטירתו וזהו שאמר לו ותנוח ומצאנו כלשון
הזה במקרא דכתיב וינוחו על משכבותם שפטירת הצדיק מנוחה היא לו מעמל העולם
הזה. ובענין זה אמר הספדן במועד קטן אל תבכו לאבדה שהלכה למנוחה ובכמה
מקומות אתה מוצא בתלמוד כשמזכירין פטירת הצדיק אומרים נח נפשיה. גם המנוחה
האמורה בדניאל אינה אלא פטירתו שהרי לא היה מבאי בית שני כדי שנאמר שעל
ביאת הארץ נאמרה לו ולא עוד אלא שסוף הפסוק מוכיח דכתיב ותעמוד לגורלך
מכלל שמנוחה זו תמורת העמידה היא והזמן השלישי אשר נאמר לו ותעמוד לגורלך
וזו היא עמידת הנפש והגוף כאחת שמא תאמ׳ שהיא עמידת הנפש בלבד לאיזה ענין
היא עומדת והלא משעת מיתה הלכה למנוחה והרי היא צרורה בצרור החיים והיכן
מעמידין אותה הא אין הכתוב מדבר אלא בשובה לגוף והרי אנו מבארין לך שאין
תחייה זו אמורה אלא בתחיית המתים לפי שנאמר בה ותעמוד לגורלך כלומר לגורל
העולה לך והע[ת] המזומן לעבודתך. ומשמע מכאן שהמתים שחיין לימות המשיח
אין כולם עומדים כאחת אלא יש מהם מוקדם הרבה ומאוחר הרבה כל אחד ואחד

לפי מעלתו אבל לעולם הבא כולם עומדים כאחת שהרי הגיע יום הדין לכולם והגיע
העת ליטו' כל אחד ואחד עונשו או שכרו הראוי לו וזהו שאמ' הכתו' כי הנה היום
בא בער כתנו[ר] והיו כל זדים וכל עושי רשעה קש וכתי' וזרחה לכם יראי שמי כו'
ועסותם רשעים כי יהיו אפר תחת כפות רגליכם ליום אשר אני עושה אמר אדני
צבאות.

33. ומאחר שבארנו שרוב הפסוקים הללו והמשניות המדברין בתחיית המתים אין
פשטן אלא בימות המשיח א"כ גם שארית הפסוקים והשמועות המדברים בתחיית
המתים ובע"ה סתם כולם נעמידם בימות המשיח ומאין לנו תחיית המתים לעה"ב
ויראה לנו שרוב המקומות שזכרו חכמים העה"ב ודאי לא דברו אלא בעה"ב באחרונה
אחרי ימות המשיח כי הא דרמי' לקמי' קראי דחפרה הלבנה אקרא דהיה אור הלבנה
כאו' החמה ומפרקי' לא קשיא כאן בעה"ז כלומר בימות המשיח והיה אור הלבנה כו'
וכאן בעה"ב וחפרה הלבנה. ולשמואל דאמר אין בין העה"ז לימות המשיח אלא
שעבוד מלכיות בלבד כאן במחנה צדיקים כאן במחנה שכינה הא למדת שאין ראוי
לקרוא העה"ב אלא העולם שאחר ימות המשיח. ואמרי' נמי לקמיה יחי ראובן לימות
המשיח ואל ימות לעה"ב.

34. והא דתנן כל ישראל יש להן חלק לעה"ב לאו באחרונה קאי והאי דאי בימות
המשיח ליכא למימר מדתני עלה דאי שאין להן חלק לעה"ב הכופר בתחיית המתים
ואמרי' בגמ' עליה וכ"כ למה תנא הוא כפר בתח"ה לפיכך לא יהא לו חלק בתחיית
המתים ואם העה"ב השנוי במשנתינו ימות המשיח הוא פסיק ותני דהכופר בתחיית
המתים אין לו חלק בימות המשיח נהי דאי מית מקמי דליתי משיח דין הוא שלא
יחיה מדה כנגד מדה אבל אם בא משיח בימיו מפני מה אין לו חלק בימות המשיח
והלא לא כפר בימות המשיח כלל ומה מדה כנגד מדה יש כאן אלא ודאי אין העה"ב
הזה השנוי במשנתינו אלא העה"ב באחרונה שאי אפשר לאדם להשיגו אלא ע"י
תחיית המתי' לפי שבין ימות המשיח והעה"ב העולם חרב כדאמרי לקמן שיתא אלפי
שני הוי עלמא וחד חרב נמצאו כל בעלי חיים מתים מתים כדכתי' כדאמרי' ואפי'
לתנא דבי אליהו דקתני מתים שעתיד הקב"ה להחיות לימו' המשיח שוב אינן חוזרים
לעפרן גם הם נמצא שאין משיגין חיי העה"ב שלא ע"י תחיית המתים לפיכך אמרו
חכמים שהכופר בתחיית המתים אין לו חלק לעה"ב לפי שאי אפשר להשיג את
העולם [הבא] אלא על ידי תחיית המתים וכיון שאין לו חלק בתחי' המתים שהרי
כפר בה נמצא שאין לו חלק לעה"ב.

35. ועוד ראיה לעה"ב השנוי במשנתינו שאינו ימות המשיח מהא דתנן שלשה
מלכים וד' הדיוטות אין להן חלק לעה"ב ואי בימות המשיח מיתי אומות העולם מאי
בעו התם דקא דייקי בגמ' בלעם הוא דלא אתי לעלמ' דאתי הא שאר גוים אחריני
אתו ועוד מדקתני עלה דור המבול אין להן חלק לעה"ב הא שאר גוים יש להם חלק
ואי בימות המשיח אמאי אלא ודאי ש"מ שאין העה"ב השנוי במשנתינו אלא יום

הדין הבא אחר ימות המשיח ודקא מייתי ליה ראיה מדכתי' לעולם ירשו ארץ שפיר
קא מייתי שהרי ישיבת הצדיקים לעה״ב מראין הדברים מאחר שיש גוף א״כ ישיבתן
לא בשמים היא אלא בארץ ומאחר שהדבר כן הוצרך לומר שיהיו חיים לעולם על
פני הארץ ועוד הוצרך לומר כי להם לבדם ניתנה הארץ כענין שנא' כי ישרים ישכנו
בארץ ותמימים יותרו בה וזהו תמורה מה שנא' ברשעים ורשעים מארץ יכרתו
ובוגדים יסחו ממנה וכענין שנ' יתמו חטאים מן הארץ.

36. וי״ל שהטובה ההיא הצפונה לצדיקים לעה״ב היא הנקראת כאן ירושת הארץ
דרך משל וזו ששני' הכופר בתחיית המתים בכלל תחיית המתים הוא כלומר שאינו
מודה בתחיית המתים ממה שנ' ונתתם ממנו תרום' ה' לאהרן. וכן רבינא ורב אשי
שהביאוהו ראיה מן הפסוקי' האמורים בדניאל הרי ביארנו למעלה שאינם מדברים
אלא בימות המשיח והמביא מהם ראיה לא נתכון להביא ראיה על תחיית המתים
השנויה במשנתינו לומר שזו היא תחיית המתים ועה״ב השנויין במשנתינו אלא לא
דברו חכמים אלא כלפי האומרים שלא נמצא רמז מן המקראו' לתחיית המתים כלל
לא בימות המשיח ולא לעה״ב לפיכך הביאו ראיה מן הפסוקים הללו להוכיח שנמצא
רמז בפסו' לתחיית המתים מ״מ אבל העה״ב נמצא כתוב במקרא בכמה מקומות
כענין שנאמר כי הנה היום בא בוער כתנור כו' וכבר ביאר לנו הנביא בפירוש בסו'
דבריו שהעה״ב שהוא יום הדין אינו בא אלא אחר ימות המשיח שנ' הנה אנכי שולח
לכם את אליה הנביא כו' ויום זה הוא יום הדין שאמרו הנביא קודם לכן באומרו
כי הנה היום בא ובוער כתנור הא למדת שביאת אליהו שהיא בימות המשיח לפני
העה״ב היא.

37. וכן ענין העה״ב נמצא מפורש בדברי רבותינו בפירוש בכמה מקומות באומרם
העה״ב אין בו לא אכילה ולא שתיה כו' והדבר ידוע שאין דברים הללו אמורים
בימות המשיח כלל שהרי יש בהן אכילה ושתיה ולא נאמרו אלא בעה״ב ומשם אתה
למד שיש בו תחיית המתים כאשר ביארנו כמה פעמים וכן אומר יחי ראובן בעה״ז
ואל ימות לעוה״ב.

38. והא דאמרי' לקמן בפרקין עולא רמי כתיב בלע המות לנצח וכתיב בה נער
בן מאה שנה ימות לא קשיא כאן בישראל כאן באומות העולם ואוקימנא בהנך דכתיב
בהו ועמדו זרים ורעו צאנכם ובני נכר אכריכם וכורמיכם על כרחיך אידי ואידי
בימות המשיח קאי דאי בעה״ב צאן הללו מה טיבם ואכרים וכורמים הללו מה טיבם
אלא בימות המשיח ועולא סבר לה כרבי יוחנן דאמר כל הנביאים לא נתנבאו כלומר
בדבר קצוב וידוע אלא לימות המשיח ומשמע דס״ל לעולא שצדיקים שזוכין לימות
המשיח אינם מתים אלא יוצאין משלום אל שלום מימות המשיח לחיי העה״ב אבל
לשמואל דאמר אין בין העה״ז לימות המשיח אלא שעבוד מלכיות בלבד יש מיתה
בימות המשיח למי שלא מת פעם אחרת והני קראי דבלע המות לנצח מוקי להו
לעה״ב וגם אנו לפי עניות דעתנו נראין דברי שמואל בעינינו דהא תנא דבי אליהו

כותיה דייקא דקתני מתים שעתיד הקב"ה להחיות בימות המשיח ולא קתני צדיקים שביטות המשיח.

39. והא דגרסי' לקמן אמ"ר חייא בן אבא אמ"ר יוחנן כל הנביאי' כולם לא נתנבאו אלא לימות המשיח אבל לעה"ב עין לא ראת' אלקים זולת' ואמ"ר חייא בר אבא אמר"י כל הנביאים כולם לא נתנבאו אלא למשיח כו'. אבל תלמידי חכמי' עצמן עין לא ראתה אלהים כו'. ואמרי' מאי עין לא ראתה אמר ריב"ל זה יין שמשומר בענביו משת ימי בראשית היא צפונה ומשומרת להן כדכתיב מה רב טובך כו' וזו היא שאמרו שמשום' בענביו ולמה נמשלה ביין לפי שאין לך דבר שמשמח לבו של אדם בעה"ז אלא יין כענין שנ' ויין ישמח לבב אנוש לפיכך נמשל' ביין לפי שהשמחה היא שמחה שאין למעלה הימנה ומה ענין המשומר בענביו לומר לך ששמחה זה לא השיגה אדם בעולם אלא כיין שמשומר בענביו שלא שלטה בו יד.

40. ויש מקומות שנא' העה"ב על ימות המשיח כאותה שאמרו חכמים בסו' דייני גזלות ודם ענב תשתה חמר אמרו לא כעה"ז העה"ב כו' דמשמע דהעה"ב יש בו אכילה ושתיה והדברים ההם אי אפשר לפתרם לפי שהן רחוקים הרבה מדרך הפתרון אבל יש להעמידן בימות המשיח שיש בהן אכילה ושתיה ואפשר לומר ששמואל לא היה מודה בה כלל וכן כל מקום שאתה מוצא בעה"ב ענין מוכיח שיש בו אכילה ושתיה אם היה דבר שאפשר לפתרו יפתר ואם לאו בידוע שלא נאמר אלא בימות המשיח ואחר שפירשנו ענין העה"ב השנוי במשנתינו לפי פשטן של דברי' ולפי מה שקבלנו מאבותינו ומרבותי' והקבלה הפשוטה בכל ישר' גם לפי שקול הדעת ומה שמדת הדין נותנת לפי עניות דעתנו נחזור לפרש שארית המשנה כפי מנהג.

Index